FOURTH EDITION

THE CO-TEACHING MANUAL

*How general education teachers and specialists
work together to educate students in an inclusive classroom*

by Dianne Basso and Natalie McCoy

TWINS
publications

Teachers Writing for Teachers

Twins Publications
P.O. Box 6364
Columbia, SC 29260-6364
(803) 782-1781
Fax (803) 787-8508
www.twinspublications.com

ISBN: 978-0-9772401-1-1

Fourth Edition
Copyright ©2009 by Twins Publications, Columbia, SC
Printed in the United States of America
All rights reserved.

TABLE OF CONTENTS

INTRODUCTION

The Co-Teaching Manual is a "how to" manual describing how general education teachers and specialists work together to educate students in an inclusive classroom. This manual provides step-by-step procedures to start and carry out a co-teaching program. It includes numerous reproducibles which are useful for monitoring student progress and facilitating communication between general education teachers and specialists and between teachers and parents.

In addition to co-teaching, the manual also discusses the use of a support class. Some students benefit from a support class (pull-out) which emphasizes IEP goals and objectives, learning strategies, social skills, study skills and homework completion.

The authors realize that the implementation of a co-teaching program as described in this manual requires planning and cooperation among general educators, specialists and administrators. The results of the authors' experiences in an inclusion program with a co-teaching component show that the effort has been worth it. Schools with co-teaching programs have reported fewer referrals, improvement in students' attitudes towards school and themselves, fewer failing grades and retentions, and an increased communication between general education teachers and specialists and between teachers and parents.

Section I

What is Co-Teaching?

RATIONALE AND DEFINITION OF CO-TEACHING

Rationale

The requirements of the No Child Left Behind Act (NCLB 2001) and the reauthorization of the Individuals with Disabilities Education Improvement Act (IDEA 2004) have brought about many changes in the delivery of instruction to students with special needs. NCLB 2001 emphasizes the accountability for learning of all students and requires all teachers to be highly qualified. IDEA 2004 further supports that students with special needs have access to the general education curriculum and ensures that these students will be taught by highly qualified teachers. One way schools and districts are meeting this challenge is through the implementation of co-teaching. While co-teaching is not a new concept, many districts are now finding it to be an effective service delivery model for increasing the achievement of students with special needs while also meeting the needs of diverse learners in the general education classroom.

Definition

*Co-teaching is an educational approach whereby general education teachers and specialists work together to deliver instruction to *all* students in an inclusive classroom. The two teachers work as partners to jointly design, plan, and implement lessons appropriate for each student. They also share the responsibility of assessing the students' mastery of the content. The general education teacher does not view the students with special needs as belonging only to the specialist, nor does the specialist view the students with special needs as his/her only responsibility. The two teachers must form a partnership in which both are responsible for meeting all students' educational needs by teaching and assisting every student in the classroom.

Co-Teaching Is:

- Co-teaching involves a general education teacher and a specialist. The specialist may be a special education teacher, a Title 1 teacher, a speech and language pathologist, a math/reading coach, an ESL teacher, a gifted education teacher or other certified personnel.

- Co-teaching classes should be heterogeneous. Co-teaching is designed to meet the educational needs of students with diverse learning abilities and styles. Careful consideration should be used when scheduling students into co-taught classes. (see *Scheduling* on pages 11-21)

- Co-teaching involves <u>shared</u> delivery of instruction and accountability. Both teachers work together to provide instruction to *all* students in the classroom.

- Co-teaching requires <u>shared</u> physical space. Both teachers use a single classroom to instruct the students. Both teachers are actively involved and remain in the classroom for the entire period of instruction.

Co-Teaching Is Not:

- Co-teaching is **not** inclusion. Inclusion is a philosophy that all students are part of the general education environment. Co-teaching is **one** part of a good inclusion program. For example, there may be a student with an IEP that is "included" in general education classes, but does not need the support of a co-taught class.

- Co-teaching is **not** "tag teaming." For example, while one teacher instructs the class, the other teacher should not sit and wait for "his/her turn."

Co-Teachers Need:

- Co-teachers need to be proficient in effective interpersonal skills. These skills include the ability to listen, actively observe, ask questions, compromise, negotiate to resolve differences, and provide feedback.

- Co-teachers need time to reach their "comfort zone."

- Co-teachers need to be patient, remain flexible and stay positive.

---

*L. Cook and M. Friend, "Co-Teaching: Guidelines for Creating Effective Practices," *Focus on Exceptional Children*, no. 28 (1995), p. 1-16.

CO-TEACHING EXPERTISE

When general education teachers and specialists collaborate, they combine the expertise of each individual teacher. They bring together the knowledge and skills each possess. The benefits to the students are innumerable. Students learn from the expertise of two professionals. In addition, administrators play a key role in the success of co-teaching.

General Educator's Expertise	Specialist's Expertise	Administrator's Expertise
• Content area • Scope and sequence of curriculum • Management strategies for large groups • Objective view of academic and social development • Pacing of curriculum • Knowledge of content standards • Maintain high expectations • Knowledge of state testing • Knowledge of additional resources for the content area	• Learning styles • Behavior modification techniques • Learning strategies • Diagnostic/ prescriptive teaching • Educational accommodations/ modifications • Identifying specific needs • Special education law • Knowledge of Individual Education Plan (IEP) • Monitoring and documenting student progress	• Creates the culture to collaborate and communicates expectations to staff • Plays key role in problem solving process by providing support and/or acting as a neutral third party • Creates logistics in school (i.e. scheduling, planning time) • Arranges for staff development • Schedules heterogeneous groups of students in co-taught classes • Recommends co-teaching partners • Observes co-teaching (see co-teaching observation forms pages 45-49) • Meets with co-teaching support groups on a regular basis (see pages 8-9)

Together these professionals ensure a creative, high-energy classroom where the needs of all students can be met. Students benefit from the expertise of two teachers. Co-teaching improves skills in students and teachers.

BENEFITS OF CO-TEACHING

These benefits were acquired through experience and numerous interviews with co-teachers, students and administrators.

• More student enthusiasm and involvement

• Increases individual instruction for students

• Less student excuses – students are held more accountable and a teacher is always available to assist

• Reduces stigma of a pull-out class, students are now included in a regular classroom

• Academic and social success for "at-risk" students

• Students appreciate having a variety of teaching styles

• Students transfer strategies such as note-taking and test-taking skills from one content area to another

• Increases teacher satisfaction in terms of the ability to meet the needs of more students in the classroom/less teacher burnout

• Shared teacher responsibility and accountability

• Reduces discipline problems

• More excitement and creativity for teachers

• More classroom grouping options (see pages 23-26)

• Professional growth for teachers

• Willingness to take more risks with grouping options, instructional methods and classroom management strategies

• Shared paperwork, phone calls, etc.

• Better and more positive communication between general education teachers and specialists

• Co-teachers provide a positive role model of cooperation for the students

• Provides enrichment, pre-teaching and re-teaching opportunities

Section II

How Do You Start a Co-Teaching Program?

A. Study the current program and determine the needs of your students.

To develop a program that best suits the students' needs, read and study co-teaching articles, books and videos. Examine your current special education program and ask:

1. Could more of our special education students in pull-out and self-contained classes be served in the general education classroom *if* they had the support of a co-teacher?

2. In what areas (subjects) do the special need's students need this additional support?

B. Provide training to educate faculty and administration about co-teaching.

Training of faculty and administration increases awareness and support of co-teaching. The training should include principals and other administrators, the teaching faculty and guidance counselors. Administrators' participation in co-teaching training allows for the development of a common vocabulary base. Administrators will learn about the many aspects of inclusion and co-teaching, and will be able to anticipate the kinds of support that will be needed to implement such a program.

The administrators can provide teachers with the support they need as well as provide release time for planning and problem solving. For the co-teaching program to succeed, everyone must be flexible, willing to try something new, and be committed to the concept of inclusion and co-teaching. They will play a key role in developing the culture to collaborate and will facilitate in the problem solving process by acting as a neutral third party.

Co-teaching training for administration and faculty should include a brief overview of the impact of the No Child Left Behind Act (NCLB 2001) and the reauthorization of the Individuals with Disabilities Education Act (IDEA 2004) on special education. These laws mandate that students, including those with disabilities, have access to the general education curriculum, are taught by highly qualified teachers and receive research based instruction. Other topics to cover are:

- Co-teaching definition
- Benefits of co-teaching
- Co-teaching expertise
- Ways to co-teach
- Co-planning
- Lesson plans
- Scheduling

Lack of administrative training and support is often a major factor in the inability to start and sustain a successful co-teaching program. Support is vital from parents, students, teachers, administration, district staff, and the school board.

C. Find other districts in your area with co-teaching programs and enlist their assistance.

Begin the search by calling your State Department of Education to find schools that have successful co-teaching programs in your area. Arrange a time for co-teachers and administrators from your school to visit and observe co-taught classes. Stay as long as you can, observe several co-taught classes and talk with the co-teachers, the students in the classes and other designated staff. Discuss the successes and challenges and ask for any material that the site-visit school has to offer. Maintain contact with teachers and administrators at that school as a support source when questions arise.

D. Schedule co-taught classes.

It takes time to develop co-teaching relationships and build successful co-teaching programs. When beginning a co-teaching program, it is important to start with teachers interested in co-teaching. (See the Co-Teaching Interest Inventory, page 74.) For example, based on students' needs, choose one or two grade levels or subject areas to co-teach the first year. Gradually, you will build upon the program's success by adding additional co-taught classes.

For more specific scheduling information, refer to Section III, How Do You Schedule, beginning on page 10.

E. Discuss grading policy.

Co-teachers and administrators should discuss a grading policy for co-taught classes. Questions to address should include:

• What is the district and school grading policy for all students?

• What is the district and school policy for assigning and recording modified grades?

• How do the students' IEPs affect grading?

• How will the final grade be determined for all students, including those with special needs?

• How will the grading policy (including any modifications) be communicated to parents?

F. Organize a co-teaching support group.

Support groups are important for the ongoing success of a co-teaching program. Co-teaching support groups are made up of all co-teaching pairs and an administrator in the school. The group meets at least four times a year for problem solving and monitoring the program's overall effectiveness.

For specific support group topics please refer to page 9.

All participants of the support group should have an agenda in advance so they can be prepared to discuss the specific topic(s). Additional staff may be invited as needed (guidance counselor, school psychologist, etc.) These suggested topics may serve as a guide to facilitate open discussion in your support groups. Assign a recorder to take notes.

1. Share successes and challenges.

2. Discuss ways to provide modifications/accommodations.

3. Discuss behavior management/discipline.

4. Share lesson plans and/or techniques that have used the six ways to co-teach effectively. Provide specific examples used for grouping.

5. Explain how co-teaching has helped the student that is struggling with academic and/or behavior problems.

6. Describe techniques for providing re-teaching in the co-taught classroom.

7. Describe strategies for providing enrichment in the co-taught classroom.

8. Discuss any ongoing concerns such as scheduling, planning and other issues that arise in the current year or as you think about planning for the next school year.

9. Provide time for the co-teachers to independently complete the **Co-Teaching Evaluation Form** on pages 72-73 and then discuss together.

10. Assess the effectiveness of the school's co-teaching program by analyzing results using curriculum-based instruction and other measurable activities.

    A. *Compare student achievement data* of students (with and without disabilities) in a co-taught classroom with a comparable class of students with and without disabilities that is not receiving co-teaching services.
    B. *Compare the discipline records* of students (with and without disabilities) in the co-taught class who have been in the same school for two or more years for longitudinal information. Compare current discipline records of students (with and without disabilities) in a co-taught classroom with a comparable class of students with and without disabilities that is not receiving co-teaching services.
    C. *Gather information* from student/teacher/parent surveys.
    B. *Decide:*
       What data will be gathered?
       Who will do it?
       How it will be done?
       When will it happen?

Section III

How Do You Schedule?

A. Determine the number of co-taught classes

Each year the number of co-taught classes changes based on students' needs. In order to determine the number of co-taught classes each year, the following points should be examined:

1. The number of students with IEPs that can be served through consultation only and do **_not_** need to be supported in co-taught classes.
   For example: A student with a mild reading disability may be served in the regular classroom with accommodations made by the general education teacher and therefore does **_not_** need to be co-taught.
2. The number of students with IEPs that need co-teaching in a specific content/subject area.
   For example: A student with a math disability may need to be in a co-taught math class, but does **_not_** need to be co-taught in other subject areas.
3. The number of students with IEPs that need co-teaching in more than one subject area.

B. Schedule co-taught classes.

Special consideration should be made by the school administration when scheduling co-taught classes. The percentage of students with IEPs in a co-taught class varies greatly based on the individual academic and behavioral needs of the students in the class.

- *For example:* A co-taught math class of 26 students may have eight students with IEPs, but these students are motivated to learn and have few accommodations/modifications. The remaining 16 students are at or above grade level and have few behavioral concerns. In this co-taught class, the teachers are able to meet the academic needs of all the students.
- *For example:* A co-taught social studies class of 26 may have four students with IEPs, but also has an ESL student and three students with academic concerns. The rest of the class is at or above grade level and has few behavioral concerns. Even with the make-up of this class, the co-teachers are still able to meet the academic expectations and the students have good social modeling.

When a co-taught class has a large percentage of students with learning and behavior challenges, teaching to the academic standards can be affected and positive role models for these students in the co-taught classroom are lacking.

- *For example:* In a co-taught language arts class of 26 students, 13 of the students have IEPs. Four of these students have significant modifications. Five have attention problems, and the remaining four have just a few accommodations. Other students in the class also have problems with reading comprehension, as well as two other students with behavior issues. This class has so many students with a variety of academic and behavior needs that the co-taught teachers are **_unable_** to keep up with the pacing and academic expectations.
- *For example:* In a co-taught science class of 26 students, four students have IEPs, five students have 504 plans, three students have been tested but did not qualify, and two have significant behavior problems. Even though this co-taught class is made up of only about 20 percent of students with IEPs, the co-teachers are **_not_** able to meet the academic needs of the class, nor does the students have good models for success.

C. Schedule co-teachers.

Experienced specialists have found they are most successful in the classroom if they limit the amount of lesson plan preparations to **three**.

- *For example:* In an elementary school, a specialist might co-teach math in one fourth grade class and co-teach reading in two 3rd grade classes. (3 different preps)
- *For example:* In a high school, a specialist might co-teach two periods of U.S. History with the same teacher and two periods of Algebra I with the same teacher. (2 different preps)

More than three different academic preparations does not allow for co-planning time which, in turn, affects the co-teachers' ability to adequately meet the needs of their students.

D. Develop the Master Schedule.

Students' needs should be put first when designing the school's Master Schedule. Therefore, co-teaching classes and co-teachers' schedules will vary from school to school and change from year to year. Specific scheduling information, including sample co-teaching schedules for the elementary, middle and high schools, are provided on pages 13-21.

A. Scheduling Co-Taught Classes in Elementary School

Elementary school scheduling is unique because of the variety of program structures at the elementary level. It is important to remember when scheduling co-taught classes that the schedule of the entire school may have to be adjusted. This adjustment is based on student needs.

In order to determine the number of co-taught classes each year, the following steps should be followed:

1. The special education teachers should make a list of the students with IEPs that can be served through consultation only (regular classroom, with some accommodations) and do **not** need the support of a co-taught class.
2. The special education teachers should then determine the students with IEPs that need co-teaching by grade and specific content/subject area. *For example:* A student with a math disability may need to be scheduled for a co-taught math class, but does not need to be co-taught in other subject areas. Some students may need co-teaching in more than one subject area.
3. The special education teachers and administration collaborate and share this information. They can now determine how many grade levels and subject areas need to be co-taught.
4. The grade levels/subjects to be co-taught are affected by student needs and the number of specialists available to co-teach. Based on this information, the administrator determines which general education teachers will be co-teaching.

The administrator (with input from the faculty) will now develop the master schedule.

- The number of preparations for each specialist should be taken into account. Studies have shown that effective co-teachers have **no more than three different academic preparations in their schedule** (see page 12).
- Common planning time should be incorporated into the schedule. Common planning time is **critical** to the success of a co-teaching program. Co-planning time allows co-teachers to develop lessons that are creative, motivating and designed to meet the needs of the diverse learners in the classroom **(see page 30).**
- Additional adjustments may need to be made in the schedule to allow for common planning time. Some schools use a floating planning period to provide common planning time during the school day. **See Sample Elementary Schedule on page 14.**
- To avoid overloading a self-contained general education class with students with special needs, there **may** need to be movement of students within the school day. *For example,* in a school with three 2nd grade classrooms, one of the teachers will co-teach language arts. During the language arts block, several students who need co-teaching will move from the other two 2nd grade classes into the co-taught class. The same number of students will move from the co-taught classroom into the other two 2nd grade classes for their language arts block. This will allow each class to maintain a balanced number of students. The administrator will need to adjust the master schedule to reflect teaching subjects at the same time.

SAMPLE ELEMENTARY CO-TEACHING SCHEDULE WITH FLOATING PLANNING PERIOD

Time	Monday	Tuesday	Wednesday	Thursday	Friday
8:00-9:00	*1st grade reading support	**Co-teach 1st grade reading	1st grade rreading support	Co-teach 1st grade reading	1st grade reading support
9:00-10:30	Co-teach 2nd grade math	Co-teach 2nd grade math	Co-teach 2nd grade math	**Plan 9-9:30 with Kindergarten and plan 9:30-10:00 with 1st grade Support**	Co-teach 2nd grade math
10:30-11:00	Support	Support	Support	Support	**Plan with 3rd grade LA**
11:00-11:30	Lunch	Lunch	Lunch	Lunch	Lunch
11:30-12:15	Co-teach Kindergarten	**Plan with 2nd grade math**	Co-teach Kindergarten	Co-teach Kindergarten	Co-teach Kindergarten
12:15-1:00	Planning	Support	Planning	Support	Planning
1:00-2:30	Co-teach 3rd language arts	Co-teach 3rd language arts	Co-teach 3rd language arts	Co-teach 3rd language arts	Co-teach 3rd language arts

This specialist serves grades K-3.

This schedule incorporates a floating planning period into the schedule.

This allows for common planning during the week with each co-teacher.

*MWF – provides intensive reading instruction to a group of students (from 8-9).

**T/Th - co-teaches with a 1st grade teacher (from 8-9).

B. Scheduling Co-Taught Classes in Middle School

1. In early spring, prior to the development of the next school year's master schedule, a transition meeting should be held. To begin the scheduling process, the middle school special education department chair should meet with the elementary school special education teacher to discuss the transition of special education students from the elementary school to the middle school.

   During this meeting:
   A. The elementary school special education teacher should submit a list of rising middle school students with IEPs that are recommended for co-taught classes. This list should include the specific subjects in which these students will need co-teaching. A separate list should include students with IEPs who do not need a co-taught class but will be included in general education classes and receive consultative services.
   B. The two teachers should discuss "reasonable" IEP accommodations for special education students in middle school.

2. Prior to the development of the next school year's master schedule, the middle school special education department should meet.

   During this meeting:
   A. The special education department should list current students with IEPs that are recommended for co-taught classes for the next school year. This list should include the specific subjects in which these students will need co-teaching. **Note:** Students with IEPs may not need to be co-taught in all subject areas. Example: A student with a math disability may only need co-teaching in math.
   B. The department should also generate a list of students with IEPs who do not need a co-taught class but will be included in general education classes and receive consultative services.

3. The special education department chairperson should now meet with the person in charge of scheduling at the middle school.

   During this meeting:
   A. The list of middle school students with IEPs recommended for co-taught classes and the specific subjects they need to be co-taught in at each grade level should be shared.
   B. The approximate number of sections for co-taught subjects at each grade level can now be determined.

4. Determine which general education teachers will be co-teaching at each grade level and subject area. Keep in mind that overloading a co-taught class with students who have special needs will not be effective. Studies indicate that an effective co-taught class should not include more than 25-30% of students with IEPs. The number of students with special needs may be less if the co-taught class also consists of several general education students that require great amounts of academic and behavioral assistance (see B on page 11).

5. The special education department and/or department chair should meet with an administrator to determine specialists' co-teaching placements. The number of preparations for each specialist should be taken into account. Studies have shown that effective co-teachers have **no more than three different academic preparations** in their schedule.

6. When developing the master schedule, common planning time for the co-teachers should be arranged. **Common planning time is critical for the success of a co-teaching program. Co-planning time allows co-teachers to develop lessons that are creative, motivating, and meet the needs of the diverse learners in the classroom.**

7. In early summer, after student schedules have been set:
   A. The special education department should meet with the person in charge of scheduling to review the schedules of all students with IEPs. Compensation for these work days should be considered.
   B. Each student's schedule should be reviewed for accuracy. Proper co-teaching placements should be verified.

8. After all students with IEPs' schedules have been reviewed and corrections have been made:
   A. A copy of rosters for the co-taught classes should be reviewed by the special education department.
   B. Special consideration should be taken to balance the number of students with IEPs and other students with behavioral and/or academic needs in each class. Changes should be made at this time to adjust and balance co-taught classes.

9. After students have received their schedules, any change requested by special education students or their parents **must be approved** by the special education department chairperson. This prevents changes from being made without the knowledge of the IEP case manager.

10. The special education department chair should be involved in the scheduling of any new student with an IEP enrolling in the middle school after the schedules have been set and/or the school year has begun. This ensures proper placement of students with IEPs.

SAMPLE MIDDLE SCHOOL CO-TEACHING SCHEDULE

Teacher A

Period	Monday	Tuesday	Wednesday	Thursday	Friday
1	Study Skills/ Support	Study Skills/ Support	Study Skills/ Support	Study Skills/ Support	Study Skills/ Support
2	Co-Teach Lang. Arts 8	Co-Teach Lang. Arts 8	Co-Teach Lang. Arts 8	Co-Teach Lang. Arts 8	Co-Teach Lang. Arts 8
3	Co-Teach Lang. Arts 7	Co-Teach Lang. Arts 7	Co-Teach Lang. Arts 7	Co-Teach Lang. Arts 7	Co-Teach Lang. Arts
4	Planning	Planning	Planning	Planning	Planning
5	Lunch	Lunch	Lunch	Lunch	Lunch
6	Co-Teach Math 7	Co-Teach Math 7	Co-Teach Math 7	Co-Teach Math 7	Co-Teach Math 7
7	Support	Support	Support	Support	Support

Teacher B

Period	Monday	Tuesday	Wednesday	Thursday	Friday
1	Co-Teach Lang. Arts 6	Co-Teach Lang. Arts 6	Co-Teach Lang. Arts 6	Co-Teach Lang. Arts 6	Co-Teach Lang. Arts 6
2	Co-Teach Math 6	Co-Teach Math 6	Co-Teach Math 6	Co-Teach Math 6	Co-Teach Math 6
3	Co-Teach Math 8	Co-Teach Math 8	Co-Teach Math 8	Co-Teach Math 8	Co-Teach Math 8
4	Study Skills/ Support	Study Skills/ Support	Study Skills/ Support	Study Skills/ Support	Study Skills/ Support
5	Support	Support	Support	Support	Support
6	Lunch	Lunch	Lunch	Lunch	Lunch
7	Support	Support	Support	Support	Support

This middle school has only 2 specialists available to co-teach.

Based on the needs of the students the two specialists will co-teach in grades 6-8 in the areas of math and language arts.

Students identified as needing additional support will also attend a study skills/support class as an elective course.

Each specialist has **three different preps.**

C. Scheduling Co-Taught Classes in High School

1. In early spring, prior to the development of the next school year's master schedule, a transition meeting should be held. To begin the scheduling process, the high school special education department chair should meet with the middle school special education department chair to discuss the transition of special education students from the middle school to the high school.

   During this meeting:
   A. The middle school department chair should submit a list of rising 9th graders with IEPs that are recommended for co-taught classes. This list should include the specific subjects in which these students will need co-teaching. A separate list should include students with IEPs who do not need a co-taught class, but will be included in general education classes and receive consultative services.
   B. Both department chairs should discuss "reasonable" IEP accommodations for special education students in high school.

2. Prior to the development of the next school year's master schedule, the high school special education department should meet.

   During this meeting:
   A. The special education department should list current 9th, 10th and 11th grade students that are recommended for co-taught classes for the next school year. This list should include the specific subjects in which these students will need co-teaching. **Note:** Students with IEPs may not need to be co-taught in all subject areas. Example: A student with a math disability may only need co-teaching in math.
   B. The department should also generate a list of students with IEPs who do not need a co-taught class but will be included in general education classes and receive consultative services.

3. The special education department chairperson should now meet with the person in charge of scheduling at the high school.

   During this meeting:
   A. The list of 9th-12th grade students with IEPs recommended for co-taught classes and the specific subjects they need to be co-taught in at each grade level should be shared.
   B. The approximate number of sections for co-taught subjects at each grade level can now be determined.

4. Determine which general education teachers will be co-teaching at each grade level and subject area. Keep in mind that overloading a co-taught class with students who have special needs will not be effective. Studies indicate that an effective co-taught class should not include more than 25-30% of students with IEPs. The number of students with special needs may be less if the co-taught class also consists of several general education students that require great amounts of academic and behavioral assistance **(see B on page 11).**

5. The special education department and/or department chair should meet with an administrator to determine specialists' co-teaching placements. The number of preparations for each specialist should be taken into account. Studies have shown that effective co-teachers have **no more than three different academic preparations** in their schedule.

6. When developing the master schedule, common planning time for the co-teachers should be arranged. **Common planning time is critical for the success of a co-teaching program. Co-planning time allows co-teachers to develop lessons that are creative, motivating, and meet the needs of the diverse learners in the classroom.**

7. In early summer, after student schedules have been set:
   A. The special education department should meet with the person in charge of scheduling to review the schedules of all students with IEPs. Compensation for these work days should be considered.
   B. Each student's schedule should be reviewed for accuracy. Proper co-teaching placements should be verified.

8. After all students with IEPs' schedules have been reviewed and corrections have been made:
   A. A copy of rosters for the co-taught classes should be reviewed by the special education department.
   B. Special consideration should be taken to balance the number of students with IEPs and other students with behavioral and/or academic needs in each class. Changes should be made at this time to adjust and balance co-taught classes.

9. After students have received their schedules, any change requested by special education students or their parents **must be approved** by the special education chairperson. This prevents changes from being made without the knowledge of the IEP case manager.

10. The special education department chair should be involved in the scheduling of any new student with an IEP enrolling in the high school after the schedules have been set and/or the school year has begun. This ensures proper placement of students with IEPs.

SAMPLE HIGH SCHOOL BLOCK A/B SCHEDULE

Thi sschool is on a block schedule. Periods 1-4 alternate days with Periods 5-8. This teacher co-teaches in the math content area only.

Period	Monday	Tuesday	Wednesday	Thursday	Friday
1A	*Geometry		Geometry		Geometry
2A	**Content Mastery		Content Mastery		Content Mastery
LUNCH					
3A	**Algebra I		Algebra I		Algebra I
4A	Planning		Planning		Plan with Geometry Co-Teacher
5B		*Geometry		Geometry	
6B		**Algebra I		Algebra I	
LUNCH					
7B		Planning		Plan with Algebra Co-Teacher	
8B		**Content Mastery		Content Mastery	

*co-teaches with the same geometry teacher - **1 prep**
co-teaches with the same algebra teacher - **1 prep
***Content Mastery is a support class (elective credit) where students learn specific study strategies and receive tutorial help. For additional information and syllabus refer to pages 55-60.

SAMPLE HIGH SCHOOL TRADITIONAL SCHEDULE

This school is on a 6 period day. The teacher co-teaches across the content area.

Period	Monday	Tuesday	Wednesday	Thursday	Friday
1	* English I	English I	English I	English I	English I
2	** Pre-Phys/ Pre-Chem	Pre-Phys/ Pre-Chem	Pre-Phys/ Pre-Chem	Pre-Phys/ Pre-Chem	Pre-Phys/ Pre-Chem
3	Plan with English I Co-Teacher	Planning	Plan with English III Co-Teacher	Planning	Plan with Pre-Phys Co-Teacher
LUNCH					
4	* English I	English I	English I	English I	English I
5	*** English III	English III	English III	English III	English III
6	**** Consultation/ Monitoring	Consultation/ Monitoring	Consultation/ Monitoring	Consultation/ Monitoring	Consultation/ Monitoring

*co-teaches with the same English I teacher - **1 prep**
co-teaches with Pre-Phys/Pre-Chem (*changes at semester*) - **1 prep
***co-teaches with English III teacher - **1 prep**
****consultation period is available for assisting in science lab classes or
  providing accommodations/modifications for students where needed

Section IV

How Do You Co-Teach?

Listed below are six ways to co-teach and examples of each. Remember, both teachers are in the classroom to serve <u>all</u> students. You may use one or more than one of the ways to co-teach during a given class period. For example, during a 50 minute class period, you may use *One Instructs, One Circulates, Parallel*, and *Team* or you may only use *Rotation* for the entire class period. The ways you co-teach will vary daily based on the lesson, the length of the class period, and how the co-teachers plan to present the material.

Do not overuse any one way of co-teaching. For example, do not use *One Instructs, One Circulates* every day, all period. This is boring for the circulating teacher and the students, and does not utilize the skills of two professionals in the classroom as true co-teachers. **Both teachers should be actively involved at all times**. For example, while one teacher is instructing the entire class, the other teacher should not be grading papers or sitting at the back of the classroom.

1. **One Instructs, One Circulates (I.C.)**
   While one teacher instructs the entire class, the other teacher circulates, helping students with particular needs or using proximity control to keep students on task.

   - *Teacher A is instructing the students on a new math concept. Teacher B walks around the room to check that students remain on task, understand the concept, are on the correct page, are taking notes, etc. If a student needs help, Teacher B is available to quietly assist.*
   - *Teacher A reviews the homework from the previous day while Teacher B circulates. Next, Teacher B introduces a new lesson while Teacher A circulates.*
   - *The circulating teacher can identify when students are not grasping a concept or need further examples or clarification. The circulating teacher can provide a non-verbal cue to the instructing teacher to re-teach a concept, slow down or provide additional examples.*

   NOTE Switch the active and passive roles to prevent one teacher being seen as the "helper." This way of co-teaching is often overused. One Instructs, One Circulates should not be used the entire class period.

2. **One Instructs, One Observes (I.O.)**
   One teacher instructs the students, while the other is systematically observing one student, a group of students or the entire class to gain specific information and for a specific purpose. This information will be analyzed together at a later time.

   - *Teacher A is teaching a math lesson, while Teacher B is observing a student's behavior in class. The information from this observation will be used to develop a behavior plan for the student.*
   - *Teacher A instructs the class, while Teacher B observes the class to adjust the seating chart.*

   NOTE Switch the active and passive roles to prevent one teacher being seen as the "helper."
   NOTE The observation should be for a specific purpose and last for a specific amount of time (i.e. 15 minutes).

3. **Rotation Grouping (R)**
   Two or more rotation groups are set up in the classroom or possibly in two separate classrooms. One teacher teaches a lesson to Group 1, while the other teacher teaches a different lesson to Group 2. Group 3, if used, is an independent group. Students rotate through the groups.

- *Teacher A, in Group 1, teaches a lesson on plant growth. Teacher B, in Group 2, conducts a science lab. Group 3, the independent group, works on a practice sheet or plays a science review game.*
- *Teacher A, in Group 1, introduces new vocabulary for a novel. Teacher B, in Group 2, returns essays and reviews the homework from the previous day. (There is not an independent group for this lesson.)*

NOTE An independent group should only be used when an activity can be completed without teacher assistance. For the independent group, the students do not have to sit together.

NOTE Individual assignments can be given to students in the independent group. This may include remediation, reteaching and enrichment exercises.

NOTE Movement, pacing and noise level should be taken into consideration when planning.

NOTE During planning, the co-teachers can predetermine the make-up of each group.

4. Parallel Grouping (P)

Divide the class into two **heterogeneous** groups with both teachers providing the same instucution.

- *Teacher A teaches two-digit addition to Group 1 using the paper/pencil method. Teacher B teaches two-digit addition to Group 2 using manipulatives. *Same lesson, different approach**
- *Teacher A reviews Chapter 3 with Group 1, while Teacher B reviews Chapter 3 with Group 2. *Same lesson, same approach**

NOTE Both teachers must know the content.

NOTE Movement, pacing and noise level should be taken into consideration when planning.

NOTE Students must be taught the same information in both groups, even if the material is presented in different ways.

5. Large Group, Small Group (LS)

Divide the class into a large group and a small group. One teacher instructs the large group, while the other teacher works with the smaller group. The smaller group may consist of students who need extra help, have been absent, need additional practice, need re-teaching or need enrichment.

- *Teacher A is instructing a small group of students that need additional review and practice. Teacher B is working with the rest of the class on an enrichment activity.*
- *Teacher A is assisting a small group of students in developing ideas for a writing assignment. Teacher B is taking the larger group to the computer lab to begin their writing assignment.*

NOTE Groups will change based on student needs. The groups should not always consist of the same students.

NOTE The same teacher should not always work with the small group.

6. Team (T)

Both teachers are active instructors. They work together to instruct the entire class. Conversation and presentation of the lesson flow seamlessly between the teachers.

- *Teacher A describes the parts of an atom, while Teacher B draws a picture or makes a model of each part as it is being described.*
- *Teacher A outlines the steps to solve an equation, while Teacher B writes each step on the overhead.*
- *Teacher B is lecturing on The Great Depression, while Teacher A is modeling note taking strategies on the overhead. Teacher B can be circulating while lecturing.*

NOTE This way of co-teaching requires good planning, respect for each other and creativity.

SAMPLE CO-TEACHING LANGUAGE ARTS LESSON

While Teacher A is doing this:	Teacher B is doing this:
Welcomes students at the door, collects last night's homework Monitors student work on opening activity	Writes opening activity on the board and tells students to list as many reasons as they can to write a letter
Leads discussion on opening activity ideas to build rationale for writing friendly letters	Lists students' ideas on overhead transparency
Explains the lesson objective — Name and describe the 5 parts of the friendly letter	Distributes the paper for writing letters
(Alternating) Explains parts 2 and 4 of the friendly letter, answers questions, monitors	(Alternating) Explains parts 1, 3 and 5 of the friendly letter, answers questions, monitors
Dictates a friendly letter to the class	After the students have finished the dictation, writes the letter correctly on the overhead, naming the correct parts
Hands out guided worksheet	Explains worksheet to students
Monitors while students complete worksheet	Monitors while students complete worksheet
Reviews by calling on students to name and describe the parts of the friendly letter	Hands out homework assignment and goes over directions

SAMPLE CO-TEACHING MATH LESSON

While Teacher A is doing this:	Teacher B is doing this:
Greets students at door	Places math warm-up problems on the overhead
Circulates to record homework and warm-up	Circulates to record homework and warm-up
Goes over warm-up and homework	Takes attendance, circulates to keep students on task
Distributes the math lab worksheet	Introduces and explains the math lab
Explains "math exercises" worksheet and does an example on the overhead	Passes out "math exercises" worksheet
Works with half of the class on the worksheet	Takes the other half of the class to another room to conduct the math lab
After a given time, switch groups and work with second half of class on the worksheet (Rotation)	After a given time, switch groups and work with second half of class on math lab (Rotation)
Class comes back together – leads discussion on worksheet	Circulates to answer questions and keeps students on task
Circulates to answer questions and keep students on task	Leads discussion on lab
Assigns homework	Checks students' homework assignment books

TIPS FOR SUCCESSFUL CO-TEACHING

✔ Utilize the skills of both teachers. Having two teachers in the classroom opens up teaching opportunities.

✔ Establish a working relationship based on mutual respect, follow through and punctuality.

✔ Be prepared. Co-planning the lesson is the key. Schedule a regular time to do this.

✔ Remain flexible. Change requires time. The first year is the hardest.

✔ Explain to parents the benefits of co-teaching.

✔ Make the co-teacher welcome in your classroom. Provide a place for his/her materials, be sure to display both names.

✔ Communicate concerns to each other. Raise disagreements while still minor and don't forget about compromise.

✔ Inform your co-teacher when you will be absent.

✔ Evaluate your co-teaching relationship and student performance on an ongoing basis.

✔ Go slowly. Learn each other's styles. Frequently discuss what works, what does not, and adjust.

Adapted and reprinted with permission from the authors, Anita DeBoer and Susan Fister from SPECIAL EDUCATOR, Jan. 1989.

10 EASY TECHNIQUES TO GUARANTEE THE FAILURE OF EDUCATIONAL PARTNERSHIPS!

✗ Act like you know it all.

✗ Sulk when your advice is not taken.

✗ Focus on your professional status.

✗ Use all available professional jargon.

✗ Be unreliable, late and inconsiderate.

✗ Appear to be aloof, formal, and superior.

✗ Spend your time telling people about your own life and accomplishments, and your busy schedule.

✗ Not planning with your co-teacher.

✗ Expect immediate results and get mad when you don't see them.

✗ AND FINALLY, act like you have all the answers.

Adapted and reprinted with permission from the authors, Anita DeBoer and Susan Fister from SPECIAL EDUCATOR, Jan. 1989.

Section V

How Do You Co-Plan?

Planning is essential for successful co-teaching. Finding time to plan during the school day is often a challenge. Ideally, both teachers would have common planning time on a daily basis. Unfortunately, this is not always the case. Listed below are suggestions of creative ways co-teachers (with administrative support) have found time to plan.

• Ask administration to schedule your planning periods at the same time.

• Ask for funding to have substitutes for planning days each grading period.

• Block special area classes (physical education, art, music, etc) at each grade level.

• Arrange to plan before or after school.

• Ask to be excused from serving on a committee or an assigned duty and spend time planning instead.

• Arrange for a common lunch time.

• Design forms that can be used to plan, and then meet together weekly to discuss.

• Use email to communicate ideas and/or plan a lesson.

• Share a notebook to write down ideas and discuss entries when planning.

• Some schools use early dismissal or late arrival days on a weekly, monthly, or once per grading period basis. The time provided on these days is used for working with colleagues.

HOW TO PLAN A LESSON WITH YOUR CO-TEACHER

Successful co-teachers meet and plan lessons on a regular basis. Co-planning takes in consideration the needs of all students. Consistent co-planning results in effective lessons, better communication, fewer misunderstandings and increased trust and respect between co-teachers. Planning also provides a time for teachers to share information about individual students. This information is helpful when planning for student success.

Refer to pages 32 and 33 for examples of completed elementary and secondary co-taught lesson plans.

As you complete a **Co-Teaching Lesson Plan Form** on page 34 or 35, consider the following questions:

1. What standard(s) will be addressed in this unit or lesson?

2. What are the main ideas all students must know?

3. What instructional methods will be used to ensure all students meet the standard(s)?

4. How can instruction be differentiated for all students?

5. How will the students be assessed for mastery of the standard(s)?

6. What is the best way for the content to be presented to the students? (***Refer to Ways to Co-Teach, Section IV, pages 23-24***)

7. What accommodations/modifications need to be made to address students' needs?

8. How will enrichment, pre-teaching and/or re-teaching be provided for students?

9. What materials and/or supplies will be needed for this unit or lesson? Who will be responsible for providing these items?

Elementary Co-Teaching Lesson Plan

Date and Standard	Co-Teaching Model	Lesson: *The Three Little Pigs*	Materials	Assessment	Homework	• Modifications • Accommodations • Enrichment
Monday		Divide the class into two groups.				
Phonemic Awareness, Word Recognition and Fluency	P	1. Each teacher reads *The Three Little Pigs* to her group and then leads a discussion on the book. Guide children in practicing voice inflections for the different pigs and the wolf. Each group dictates answers to questions and decides what lesson was learned in the story.	*The Three Little Pigs* Questions	Observation and responses to questions	None	Read *The Three Little Pigs* to Janey in advance of the lesson. Help her to formulate an answer to what lesson was learned.
	T	2. Both groups come together and present their answers. Both teachers circulate.	Shapes, cardboard bricks, glue, papers raffia, straws			Remind John to take his behavior contract out.
	R	3. Divide into three rotation groups. Group 1: Teacher A works with students to glue shapes and raffia on paper to make a straw house. Group 2: Teacher B works with students to glue shapes to make a stick house. Group 3: Independent: Students play together with large cardboard "bricks" to make a brick house.	Action song words			Have Mrs. Smith preteach the action song to Janey, Susan and Hunter
	T	Teacher A leads class in song as Teacher B demonstrates motions.				

IC - *Instruct, Circulate*   **IO** - *Instruct, Observe*   **R** - *Rotation*   **P** - *Parallel*   **LS** - *Large Group/Small Group*   **T** - *Team*

Secondary Co-Teaching Lesson Plan

Date and Standard	Co-Teaching Model	Lesson: Teacher A	Teacher B	Materials	Assessment	Homework	• Modifications • Accommodations • Enrichment
October 4 Government	T IC R (10 minutes each group) T LS	1. Pass out study guide and assignment for independent group 2. Divide the class into two groups 3. Work with Group I to go over the rubric Independent Group will work to brainstorm research ideas with student group facilitator (on chart paper) 4. Place the 3 groups brainstorming ideas on the wall charts 5. Facilitate students in narrowing down and choosing project idea	1. Review directions for groups 2. Assist in movement into groups 3. Work with Group II on organizing a research packet including check-off list 4. Explain directions 5. Work with Dallas, Jack and Brittany to choose a project idea	Rubrics Packet Chart Paper Markers	Completed brainstorming charts	Begin research project	James and Stephen should not be in same group. Have Dallas, John, Amanda and Brittany in Group I with Stephen, Josh, Shante and Ashley. Jason will have access to a laptop to record info.

IC - *Instruct, Circulate*   IO - *Instruct, Observe*   R - *Rotation*   P - *Parallel*   LS - *Large Group/Small Group*   T - *Team*

Co-Teaching Lesson Plan - Daily

Date and Standard	Co-Teaching Model	Lesson	Materials	Assessment	Homework	• Modifications • Accommodations • Enrichment

IC - *Instruct, Circulate*   IO - *Instruct, Observe*   R - *Rotation*   P - *Parallel*   LS - *Large Group/Small Group*   T - *Team*

Co-Teaching Lesson Plan - Weekly

Subject: _____

Period/Tiime: _____

Co-Teachers: _____

Week of: _____

Date and Standard	Co-Teaching Model	Lesson	Materials	Assessment	Homework	• Modifications • Accommodations • Enrichment
Monday						
Tuesday						
Wednesday						
Thursday						
Friday						

IC - *Instruct, Circulate*   **IO** - *Instruct, Observe*   **R** - *Rotation*   **P** - *Parallel*   **LS** - *Large Group/Small Group*   **T** - *Team*

The **Co-Teaching Worksheet** should be completed with your co-teacher <u>prior</u> to the start of co-teaching. The **Co-Teaching Worksheet** encourages discussion of educational beliefs, expertise and classroom management. The completion of this worksheet eliminates many misunderstandings that could occur without open communication and discussion prior to teaching together.

Co-teachers should complete and review this worksheet each year they co-teach together. Below is a sample of the **Co-Teaching Worksheet.** Please refer to pages 83-86 for a clean copy of the **Co-Teaching Worksheet.**

CO-TEACHING WORKSHEET

It is recommended that both teachers complete this worksheet together <u>prior</u> to their co-teaching experience. Reviewing procedural matters now will help to avoid miscommunication and frustration that may arise during the school year.

1. Discuss your philosophy about teaching students with special needs in a general education classroom.

_____

_____

_____

2. Explain your interest in co-teaching.

_____

_____

_____

3. Share some of the co-teaching responsibilities you would like to have.

_____

_____

_____

4. Discuss your biggest concern(s) about co-teaching.

_____

_____

_____

5. What are your goals for this co-taught class?

_____

_____

_____

6. Talk about instructional expectations. Discuss the standards, the scope and sequence, and pacing for the course. **Note:** Each co-teacher should be provided a copy of the course standards and a teacher's edition of the textbook.

_____

_____

_____

7. List all correspondence which will use both teachers' names. **Example:** notes to parents, newsletters, syllabi, schedules, report cards, etc.

_____

_____

_____

8. Decide on a designated place or desk for the co-teacher (coming into the classroom) to keep his/her materials.

_____

_____

_____

9. How will parents be informed that their student will be in a co-taught class? (See **Co-Teaching Parent Letter,** page 82)

_____

_____

_____

10. How will each of you be introduced to the students? What can you do to convey to the students that two professional teachers are in the classroom working together? **Example:** the use of "we" instead of "I"

_____

_____

_____

11. How will parental contacts be made? **Example:** Who will return phone calls and e-mails, attend parent/teacher conferences, and so forth?

   _____

   _____

   _____

12. How will IEP accommodations/modifications be monitored? Where will the information about the students' accommodations/modifications be kept? **Example:** specified binder, grade book, file folder, etc.

   _____

   _____

   _____

13. How and when will you plan? *This time is very important, so schedule now before your calendars are full.* (See **Finding Time to Plan**, page 30).

   _____

   _____

   _____

14. What are your pet peeves? We all have a least one! **Example:** If you do not want students to use pens on quizzes and tests, state it; if you cannot stand students chewing gum in class, let it be known.

   _____

   _____

   _____

15. How will you notify your co-teacher that you will be absent? What will the substitute be expected to do? **Note:** An absent co-teacher should always be provided a substitute. This substitute should not be pulled from a co-taught class to cover another class.

   _____

   _____

   _____

16. Discuss paperwork responsibilities. These may include:

• attendance procedures _____

• discipline referrals _____

• progress reports/newsletters to parents _____

• bulletin boards _____

• copying papers _____

• other _____

17. Discuss the grading and recording of written assignments, quizzes and tests.

_____

_____

_____

18. Discuss classroom rules and how they will be enforced.

_____

_____

_____

19. Discuss daily class routines and procedures for students:

• leaving the class for water and restroom_____

• late to class _____

• asking questions in class _____

• turning in written assignments _____

• sharpening pencils_____

• lining up (elementary)_____

• walking down the hall (elementary) _____

• taking make-up quizzes and tests _____

• getting missed assignments_____

• turning in late assignments _____

• transitioning within classroom (noise level) _____

20. Discuss the acquisition and utilization of supplies and equipment needed for the classroom.

_____

_____

_____

21. How will you resolve differences? Some differences of opinion are normal. **Have a plan to communicate concerns while they are still small.**

_____

_____

_____

22. Schedule a date each grading period to complete an evaluation. Discuss the results and adjust as needed. (See **Co-Teaching Evaluation,** pages 72-73)

_____

_____

_____

Section VI

How Do You Evaluate and Observe Co-Teaching?

EVALUATION AND OBSERVATION

In order to improve your co-teaching and co-teaching relationships, it is important to evaluate them regularly. Co-teachers should complete the **Co-Teaching Evaluation Form**, (pages 72-73) each grade period. These forms are filled out **independently**. Upon completion the co-teachers meet and discuss the results and make adjustments accordingly.

When administrators observe a co-taught class, they should use a tool that reflects good co-teaching practices. Formal and informal **Co-Teaching Observation Forms** can be found on pages 77-81.

CO-TEACHING EVALUATION FORM

Teacher completing form _____ Date_____

Co-teacher's name_____ Grading period_____

This form should be completed, **independently,** by both co-teachers each grading period. The co-teachers should meet, discuss the results and make adjustments accordingly. (clean copy on pages 72-73)

Respond to each statement by circling Y (for yes) and N (for no)

1.	We plan on a regular basis.	Y	N
2.	We both participate in the planning of the lessons.	Y	N
3.	The special education teacher has a copy of the course curriculum standards and a teacher's manual.	Y	N
4.	We follow classroom rules and routines.	Y	N
5.	Both teachers share in the behavior management of the classroom.	Y	N
6.	We use a variety of classroom management strategies.	Y	N
7.	We share daily record keeping duties.	Y	N
8.	We share in the grading of quizzes, tests, homework, etc.	Y	N
9.	We assess students in a variety of ways.	Y	N
10.	Both teachers demonstrate knowledge of individual student's modifications and accommodations.	Y	N
11.	IEP modifications/accommodations have been followed and documented.	Y	N
12.	We use a variety of instructional strategies to promote the success of all students.	Y	N
13.	We use a variety of ways to co-teach. (i.e. rotation, parallel, grouping, team)	Y	N
14.	Both teachers work with all students.	Y	N
15.	We have successfully grouped disabled students with non-disabled peers.	Y	N
16.	Both teachers participate in the instruction of the students on a daily basis.	Y	N
17.	We notify each other in advance in the event of an absence.	Y	N
18.	Both teachers remain in the classroom the entire class period.	Y	N
19.	We share parental contact responsibilities.	Y	N
20.	We consistently address the class as "we" instead of "I".	Y	N

21. Both names are listed on written correspondence. (syllabi,   Y   N
notes to parents, schedules, newsletters, etc.)

22. Each teacher has a designated place or area in the classroom in which   Y   N
to keep meterials.

23. Students see us as equal teaching partners.   Y   N

24. Administrators see us as equal teaching partners.   Y   N

List 3 strengths of your co-teaching partnership.

1. _____

2. _____

3. _____

List 2 ideas for improvement in your co-taught class during the next grading period.

1. _____

2. _____

Observing a co-taught class is different than observing a class taught by one teacher; both teachers share in the delivery of instruction. The observer should use a form that shows evidence that both teachers have been involved in planning, instructing and assessing all students in the co-taught class. Below is a sample of a formal Co-Teaching Observation. For a clean copy of the **Co-Teaching Observation Form,** see pages 77-80.

CO-TEACHING OBSERVATION FORM/FORMAL

Co-Teacher _____ Co-Teacher _____

Subject _____ Grade _____

Observer _____

Date and Time of Observation_____ Date and Time of Follow-up Conference_____

It is recommended that both co-teachers receive a copy of this form in a pre-observation conference. At that time, the observer should inform the teachers on how this form will be used. Note: Every element listed may not be observed during one lesson. A co-teaching relationship develops gradually and is based on mutual trust and respect. Co-teachers continually develop their skills as they work with each other.

<table>
<tr><td>0 - not observed</td><td>1 - somewhat evident</td><td>2 - clearly evident</td></tr>
</table>

I. PLANNING/PREPARATION

A. Both teachers can provide evidence of parity. (a desk or place for each teacher to keep materials, both names on materials sent home, on class rosters, syllabi, newsletters, on the door, etc.)	0	1	2
B. Both teachers can provide the most recent completed copy of the **Co-Teaching Evaluation Form,** page 72.	0	1	2
C. Both teachers can provide a copy of IEP accommodations/modifications for students in their class.	0	1	2
D. Both teachers were involved in the development of the lesson plan.	0	1	2

CO-TEACHING OBSERVATION FORM con't.

0 - not observed   1 - somewhat evident   2 - clearly evident

I. PLANNING/PREPARATION, con't

The lesson plan includes:

E. Appropriate academic standards and objectives for lessons consistent with the state's curriculum guidelines	0	1	2
F. Use of more than one way of co-teaching (refer to **Ways to Co-Teach Quick Reference**, page 47)	0	1	2
G. Planning for varied instructional strategies	0	1	2
H. Evidence that both teachers will be actively involved with instruction	0	1	2
I. Evidence of adaptations for individual student's needs (both enrichment and remediation)	0	1	2
J. Evidence of accommodations/modifications	0	1	2
K. Appropriate and clear assessments of student learning with adaptations, as needed	0	1	2

II. CLIMATE FOR LEARNING

Both teachers' performance demonstrates a shared responsibility for:

A. Classroom rules and procedures resulting in effective use of instructional time	0	1	2
B. Effective management of classroom behavior	0	1	2
C. Promoting and modeling respectful interaction among the students, between teachers and students and between the co-teachers	0	1	2
D. Communicating high expectations for all students through support and encouragement	0	1	2
E. Ensuring that all students are engaged in meaningful work throughout the class time	0	1	2
F. Both teachers work with all students; the classroom environment would make it difficult to identify students with disabilities from their non-disabled peers.	0	1	2

0 - not observed   1 - somewhat evident   2 - clearly evident

III. INSTRUCTIONAL PRACTICES

During instruction, both teachers:

A. Use "we" and "us" instead of "I" and "my"	**0**	**1**	**2**
B. Are actively involved in the instruction of all students with communication and instruction flowing freely between the co-teachers	**0**	**1**	**2**
C. Use a variety of instructional strategies to promote the success of all students ☐ individualized instruction ☐ grouping strategies 　　(refer to **Ways to Co-Teach Quick Reference** listed below) ☐ manipulatives/technology ☐ projects ☐ peer teaching ☐ direct instruction ☐ other＿＿＿＿＿＿＿＿＿＿＿＿＿＿＿＿	**0**	**1**	**2**

WAYS TO CO-TEACH QUICK REFERENCE

One Instructs, One Circulates (I,C)

Teacher A manages the overall classroom and oversees instruction. Teacher B circulates answering questions, getting the attention of students back on lesson, helping an individual, etc.

One Instructs, One Observes (I,O)

One teacher manages the overall classroom and oversees instruction. The other teacher plays a passive role, but is observing one student, a group of students or even the whole class for a specific purpose of gaining information and for a specific amount of time. This information will be analyzed together.

Rotation (R)

Students rotate through stations. Teacher A works at one station presenting information or an activity. Teacher B works at another station presenting different information or activity. One station is for independent work.

Parallel (P)

Co-teachers are both teaching the same information, but they divide the class.

Large Group, Small Group (L,S)

The class is divided. Teacher A instructs a large group in a planned lesson and Teacher B leads a small group in another lesson or the same lesson taught at a different level or for a different purpose.

Team (T)

Both teachers are active instructors. They work together to instruct the entire class. Conversation and presentation of the lesson flow seamlessly between the teachers.

CO-TEACHING OBSERVATION FORM con't.

0 - not observed   1 - somewhat evident   2 - clearly evident

III. INSTRUCTIONAL PRACTICES

During instruction, both teachers:

D. Provide guided practice (i.e. modeling note-taking during instruction)	**0**	**1**	**2**
E. Move about the classroom	**0**	**1**	**2**
F. Assist students with and without disabilities	**0**	**1**	**2**
G. Adapt the instruction to a variety of learning styles (visual, auditory, kinesthetic, tactile)	**0**	**1**	**2**
H. Know content of the lesson	**0**	**1**	**2**
I. Are comfortable with their presentation of the content	**0**	**1**	**2**
J. Group students with disabilities with their non-disabled peers	**0**	**1**	**2**
K. Re-teach students who need extra help	**0**	**1**	**2**
L. Provide materials that are adapted to meet individual student needs	**0**	**1**	**2**
M. Demonstrate appropriate pacing of instruction	**0**	**1**	**2**
N. Provide accommodations/modifications for students as needed	**0**	**1**	**2**
O. Ask a variety of questions using higher order thinking skills	**0**	**1**	**2**

IV. ONGOING ASSESSMENT STRATEGIES

The co-teachers use a variety of ongoing assessment strategies to fairly and accurately evaluate the real learning of the students. These may include: ☐ intervention activities to re-teach objectives ☐ group or individual questioning ☐ teacher-made and standardized quizzes/tests with appropriate adaptations and accommodations ☐ students working at the board ☐ written or oral assignments ☐ projects ☐ labs ☐ other _____	**0**	**1**	**2**

Follow Up Conference and Signatures

_____
Teacher's Signature and Date

_____
Teacher's Signature and Date

_____
Observer's Signature and Date

CO-TEACHING OBSERVATION FORM/INFORMAL
(SIX IN SIX MINUTES)

Observer _____ Date _____

Co-Teachers_____ Subject/Period _____

NOTES FROM OBSERVATION

0 - not observed   1 - somewhat evident   2 - clearly evident

I. Co-teachers have planned together.   0   1   2

2. Teachers use "we" and/or "us."   0   1   2

3. Both teachers are involved in instruction.   0   1   2

4. Students are engaged in learning.   0   1   2

5. Both teachers work with all students.   0   1   2

6. Ways to co-teach observed:

☐ One Instructs, One Circulates

☐ One Instructs, One Observes

☐ Rotation

☐ Parallel

☐ Small Group, Large Group

☐ Teaming

Additional Notes:

Section VII

What Are Some Classroom Accommodations/ Modifications?

INSTRUCTIONAL ACCOMMODATIONS AND MODIFICATIONS

This section lists effective modifications and accommodations for working with the diverse needs of students in the regular classroom. Many of these are simply good teaching strategies. These strategies should be matched with students' learning styles and ability levels. Some students will have accommodations and modifications listed on their Individualized Education Programs (IEP's).

1. Give clear oral and written instructions.

2. Provide study guides as a review before tests.

3. Provide study questions/guides for upcoming chapters or class discussions.

4. Use preview questions for media presentation.

5. Allow students to tape record class lectures and/or discussions.

6. Highlight the most essential information on handout material.

7. Provide outlines of videotape content.

8. Break lengthy projects down into short tasks.

9. Change activities before the student's attention span is gone.

10. Give students several alternatives in obtaining and reporting information - tapes, interviews, experiences, make charts, posters, hands-on activities.

11. Reduce the amount of material the student must copy from the board.

12. Allow access to computer for written work.

13. Provide new vocabulary list prior to instruction.

14. Pair low-ability students with peer tutors for study, review and/or test preparation.

15. Allow students to independently view films, listen to tapes, etc. outside of class.

16. Tape record content from text(s).

17. Provide seating in close proximity to activity to keep student focused.

18. Contact the Special Education Teacher if the student begins to fall behind and needs additional help.

19. Provide notes or note taking assistance for students who are slower in writing skills.

20. Read printed material aloud.

21. Use assistive technology.

22. Provide extra time to complete assignments.

23. Allow calculator use for student with identified math disability.

24. Spelling should be counted only if that is the skill being tested.

25. Academic progress reports are given to parents on a regular time interval.

26. Reduce amount of work required to show mastery of concept.

TEST TAKING ACCOMMODATIONS

1. Provide oral administration or tape recorded tests.

2. Make old tests available as study guides.

3. Read words aloud or restate questions on tests as needed.

4. Allow students to access a tape recorder or word processor to answer essay questions.

5. Allow the student additional time to complete the test.

6. Space the items on the test page to avoid crowding.

7. Break up test administration into shorter sessions.

8. Allow students to write on the test instead of using answer sheets.

Section VIII

How Do You Provide Additional Support for Students in Co-Taught Classes?

SUPPORT CLASS (PULL-OUT)

In addition to co-taught classes and other general education classes, some students are served in a support class. A support class may consist of teacher-directed instruction in study skills, as well as support for the students in their general education classes. The exact format of the class should be based on the needs of the students.

For those students who need additional support outside of content courses, a support class and its varied curriculum helps the student "keep it all together," thus reducing the number of failures that might occur in the general education classroom. Not all students in a co-taught class will be served in a support class.

A typical support class may include these curriculum and instructional guidelines:

A. IEP goals and objectives

1. Address specific IEP goals/objectives for each student

2. Document student progress on goals and objectives

B. Basic organizational skills

1. Notebook organization with weekly notebook check using **Notebook Organization Point Sheet,** page 94.

2. Use of an agenda or **Homework Assignment Sheet,** page 90. Student records homework for all subjects. The support teacher monitors homework completion for the student's content area subject using the **Agenda Check Sheet,** page 68.

3. Time management——setting time priorities, time to complete homework, studying for tests, and working on long range projects

C. Study skills

1. Understanding parts of the textbook

2. Reading the text for meaning, main ideas, outlining the chapters and using the book to study for tests

3. Completing exercises and practice in reading and following directions

4. Note taking skills

5. Test taking skills and methods to reduce test anxiety

6. Sentence and paragraph writing skills

7. Memory skills

8. Proofreading skills

9. Listening skills

D. Academic assistance for content area classes

1. Preteaching vocabulary or concepts

2. Providing additional time for accommodations/modifications

Organize your binders to contain everything needed to be a successful student. Complete the following steps to organize each binder.

1. In the front of each binder, place a copy of your daily schedule and class syllabus (if applicable).

2. Using index tab dividers, separate and label each binder into sections, as directed by each content area teacher.

3. Place all loose assignments, worksheets, tests, etc. in the correct section of the binder as soon as you receive them.

4. **Date everything!** This includes all notes, assignments, tests, homework, etc. This will make it much easier to find information and to study for tests.

5. Keep plenty of paper in each binder at all times. This will prevent lost work due to writing in the wrong binder or section because you ran out of paper.

A notebook organization point sheet can be used to evaluate organizational skills.

NOTEBOOK ORGANIZATION POINT SHEET

Name _____

Date _____

Criteria: Notebook present_____
(25 points)

Criteria: Dates on work _____
(20 points)

Criteria: Pages in order _____
(20 points)

Criteria: All papers secure _____
(10 points)

Criteria: Study skills noted_____
(25 points)

Total score: _____/100 points

Comments: _____

_____

_____

Name _____

Date _____

Criteria: Notebook present_____
(25 points)

Criteria: Dates on work _____
(20 points)

Criteria: Pages in order _____
(20 points)

Criteria: All papers secure _____
(10 points)

Criteria: Study skills noted_____
(25 points)

Total score: _____/100 points

Comments: _____

_____

_____

MIDDLE/HIGH SCHOOL

Teacher's Name _____Room_____

Planning Period _____School Telephone_____

School Year _____

A. Instructional Goals:
   1. To achieve success in all content area classes
   2. To develop and reinforce organizational and study skills
   3. To promote student responsibility and personal life skills

B. Textbook: None

C. Fees: None

D. Organization of Instruction:
   1. The first half of each class period will be a teacher-directed lesson addressing study skills, organizational skills and individual needs.
   2. The second half of each class period will be independent study for content area classes. (Teacher direction, guidance and assistance will be available to each student.)
   3. Each student's progress will be monitored routinely.
   4. The individual needs and goals of each student will be addressed and considered in all aspects of this course.

E. Student Responsibilities:
   1. Each student is responsible for bringing all necessary materials to class daily. The student will be responsible for organizing content area notebooks and completing homework assignment agendas.
   2. Active participation in all teacher-directed and independent activities is required.
   3. Each student is expected to use this time in class and the assistance available to ensure his/her academic success.
   4. Each student is expected to behave in an appropriate manner and show consideration for each person in the classroom.

F.   Grading Procedures:

Interim and nine weeks' grades will be computed as follows:

100%   1/3 daily work and/or homework
              1/3 content notebook check and completion of homework assignment sheet
              1/3 tests

1st and 2nd semester grades will be computed as follows:

80%   Average of 1st and 2nd (or 3rd & 4th) nine weeks' grades
20%   Exam grade

Yearly grades will be computed as follows:

              Average of 1st and 2nd semester grades

G.   Sequence of Instruction:

First Semester
1. Notebook Organization
2. Homework Assignment Sheet
3. IEP Self Advocacy
4. Parts of a Textbook
5. Time Management
6. Memory
7. Test Taking Strategies
8. Listening Skills

Second Semester
10. Notetaking/Outlining Skills
11. Writing/Editing Skills
12. SQ3R Study Strategies

H.   Text:

Study Tools: A Comprehensive Study Skills Curriculum by Basso and McCoy, Twins Publications.

TEACHER ORGANIZATION

A co-teacher may be traveling room to room throughout the school building. Organizing all essential forms, supplies, and papers in one notebook is helpful. Use index tabbed dividers to label and separate the different sections. This notebook is used as a model when discussing organization with students.

A typical three-ring notebook might be organized in this way:

1. **Calendar/School Agenda**
   Calendars located in the front of the notebook help to keep track of meetings, birthdays, assigned duties and other important dates.

2. **Co-Taught and Support Classes**
   Label and divide each co-taught and support class into sections. In these sections include information for the class, student information and other pertinent data.

3. **Student Information**
   In this section include **Documentation of Parental Contact,** page 89, **IEP Classroom Accommodations/Modifications,** page 92 and **Student Information,** page 99. Also include their schedule and/or teacher assignment.

4. **The Master Schedule**
   This schedule lists the teaching schedule of all the teachers in the school, their location, and their planning period. This is especially valuable for meetings when consulting with students or teachers.

5. **Forms**
   This section contains blank copies of any forms that may be needed throughout the school day.

6. **Supplies**
   Carry pens, pencils, highlighters, rubber bands, paper clips, sticky notes, calculator, hall passes, etc. In short, any item that you can carry and will keep you from retracing your steps is put in your notebook.

7. **Student/Parent School Handbook**
   Keep a copy of the school handbook to refer to as needed.

Section IX

What Are Some Terms You Need To Know?

1. **Co-Teaching**
   A service delivery option in which two educational professionals deliver instruction in a classroom made up of students with IEPs and non-disabled students. Both teachers work together to instruct <u>all</u> students in the class. These teachers plan together to provide a variety of ways for diverse learners to meet their educational needs. For additional information please refer to pages 3, 23-24.

2. **Exceptionality Areas**
   IDEA has categorized the following disabilities for special education services:
   - visual impairment
   - speech and language impairment
   - auditory impairment
   - deaf/blind
   - autism
   - developmental disabilities (mental retardation)
   - multiple disabilities
   - orthopedic impairment
   - specific learning disabilities
   - emotional/behavior disorder
   - traumatic brain injury
   - multi-sensory impairment
   - serious health impairments

3. **Inclusion or Inclusive Education**
   Refers to the philosophy/policy of integrating students with special needs into general education classes to the maximum extent appropriate in the school they would otherwise attend.

4. **Individualized Education Plan (IEP)**
   A written education plan that must be developed annually for all students receiving special education services. It is a road map for the instruction of the student with special needs.

5. **Individuals with Disabilities Education Act (IDEA)**
   IDEA is a federal law that was originally passed in 1997 and further revised in 2004. This law guarantees a free appropriate education for students with special learning needs in the least restrictive environment.

6. **Least Restrictive Environment (LRE)**
   LRE is a legal term defined under federal and state special education laws and regulations. This clause places responsibility on the school district to educate, to the maximum extent appropriate, disabled students with non-disabled students.

7. **No Child Left Behind Act of 2001**

This federal law contains these basic education reform principles: increases the standards for student accountability for states, school districts and schools, increases flexibility and local school board control, provides more educational options for parents when choosing which schools their children will attend, and places the emphasis on educational methods that are built on scientifically- based research.

8. **Section 504 of the Rehabilitation Act of 1973**

This Act is enforced by the U.S. Office of Civil Rights and provides qualified persons protection from discrimination on the basis of disability in all programs and activities receiving federal financial assistance. <u>This is not a special education law</u>. 504 plans are a general education service.

9. **Support Class (Pull Out)**

In addition to co-taught classes and other general education classes, some students with special needs are served in a support class. A support class may consist of teacher directed study skills instruction, as well as support for the student in their general education classes. The exact format of the class will be dependent on the needs of the students, school, and district.

Section X

Reproducible Forms

This section provides you with numerous forms. You may not use them all, but what you do use will help you keep track of the changing learning needs of the students. These forms are used to show that you expect your students to succeed, and you will do what you can to bring about that success.

Monitoring Sheets

Provide additional support for your students through monitoring sheets. Initiation of these sheets may come at the request of a parent or the school. These sheets may be used on a daily or weekly basis, according to individual needs.

1. The **Weekly Assignment Sheet** should list assignments, future tests, projects and other class requirements. This should *not* take the place of the student completing a daily homework agenda or **Homework Assignment Sheet.**

2. The **Daily Monitoring Report** is used when a parent requests to have a student monitored in a particular class on a *daily* basis. The student can be responsible for having this form completed and for taking it home.

3. The **Weekly Progress Report** is used when a parent requests to have a weekly report from a teacher. It can be the student's responsibility to ask the teacher to complete the form and to take the completed form home to share with his parents.

4. The **Daily Observation Sheet** provides for specific documentation of a student as needed. This form may be completed by the teacher when a student is having discipline problems or is exhibiting unusual behavior in class. It can also be used when a student is being referred to the special education program as documentation for a parent meeting, and by co-teachers using **one instructs, one observes.**

Maintaining Contact with General Education Teachers and Parents

The following forms provide ways to share information and study skills recommendations.

1. **IEP Classroom Accommodations/Modifications** provides a reproducible form for specialists to forward information to the general education teacher and administration regarding the characteristics and needs of certain students. Complete these and distribute them to the students' teachers at the beginning of the school year.

2. The **Student Progress Report, Progress Report for Parents** and **IEP Annual Review Progress Report** are sent to the students' general education teacher at the appropriate times during the year.

3. The **Request for Consultation Letter and Form** is used by general education teachers to request the consultation services of the special education teacher.

4. **Documentation of Parental Contact** is used to document phone calls made to the parent or meetings held throughout the year. One form is kept for each student on your caseload.

5. **Other Forms/Letters**

   - Agenda Check Sheet
   - Co-Teaching Evaluation
   - Co-Teaching Interest Inventory
   - Co-Teaching Lesson Plan
   - Co-Teaching Observation Forms
   - Co-Teaching Parent Letter
   - Co-Teaching Worksheet
   - Consultative Program Evaluation
   - Consultative Student Progress Report
   - Introduction to Parent Letter
   - Itinerant Documentation Letter
   - Notebook Organization Point Sheet
   - Notification of Parent Meeting
   - Support Class Program Evaluation
   - Student Information Sheet
   - Test Preparation Form

QUICK REFERENCE OF FORMS

AGENDA CHECK SHEET

Student's Name _____

DATE	AGENDA ON DESK 10 points	SUBJECTS WRITTEN IN AGENDA 10 points	LEGIBLE 10 points	HOMEWORK WRITTEN FOR EACH SUBJECT 70 points	TOTAL POINTS 100

CONSULTATIVE DOCUMENTATION LETTER

TO: Teachers of Consultative Students

FROM: Learning Strategies Department

DATE:

RE: Consultative Documentation Forms

A student with an IEP (Individualized Education Plan) is required to receive direct/indirect services. Many of our special education students are served under the consultative model. This means they are not seen by a special education teacher on a daily basis. We will be sending a form to you to document services provided. We will use these forms when working with the student or communicating with the parent, and they will be placed in the student's IEP folder. This will be legal documentation for us, as well as for you, of services and help provided to this student. We realize everyone is overloaded with paperwork, but we know this will help all of us work together to better serve and educate the consultative special education students at _____.

(School's Name)

CONSULTATIVE PROGRAM EVALUATION

(to be completed by student)

Name (optional) _____

1. Do you feel you are getting the help you need?

   ☐ Yes   ☐ No

   Explain _____

   _____

2. What do you like about the Consultative program? _____

   _____

   _____

   _____

3. What do you feel has helped you this year?

   _____ weekly contact with specialists

   _____ classes with co-teachers

   _____ accommodations in classes (ex: extended test-taking time)

   _____ progress reports

   _____ other (Please explain) _____

4. How would you improve the Consultative program? _____

   _____

   _____

   _____

CONSULTATIVE STUDENT PROGRESS REPORT

Teacher completing form: _____ Class: _____

Student's Name: _____ Date due: _____

Return to: _____

Directions: Please circle the number that best describes the student in each category.

Category 1: **Behavior in class**

1	2	3	4	5
POOR		SATISFACTORY		EXEMPLARY

Comments: _____

_____

Category 2: **Homework Completion**

1	2	3	4	5
LITTLE		MOST		ALL

Comments: _____

_____

Category 3: **Classwork Completion**

1	2	3	4	5
LITTLE		MOST		ALL

Comments: _____

_____

Category 4: **Stays on Task**

1	2	3	4	5
RARELY		MOST TIMES		ALL

Comments: _____

_____

Category 5: **Estimated Grade**

1	2	3	4	5
F	D	C	B	A

Comments: _____

_____

Additional accommodations/modifications needed for this student: _____

FOR CONSULTANT'S USE ONLY

Student Signature _____

Consultant Signature _____

Date reviewed: _____

CO-TEACHING EVALUATION FORM

Teacher completing form _____Date_____

Co-teacher's name_____Grading period_____

This form should be completed, **<u>independently</u>**, by both co-teachers each grading period. The co-teachers should meet, discuss the results and make adjustments accordingly.

Respond to each statement by circling Y (for yes) and N (for no)

1. We plan on a regular basis.	Y	N
2. We both participate in the planning of the lessons.	Y	N
3. The special education teacher has a copy of the course curriculum standards and a teacher's manual.	Y	N
4. We follow classroom rules and routines.	Y	N
5. Both teachers share in the behavior management of the classroom.	Y	N
6. We use a variety of classroom management strategies.	Y	N
7. We share daily record keeping duties.	Y	N
8. We share in the grading of quizzes, tests, homework, etc.	Y	N
9. We assess students in a variety of ways.	Y	N
10. Both teachers demonstrate knowledge of individual student's modifications and accommodations.	Y	N
11. IEP modifications/accommodations have been followed and documented.	Y	N
12. We use a variety of instructional strategies to promote the success of all students.	Y	N
13. We use a variety of ways to co-teach. (i.e. rotation, parallel, grouping, team)	Y	N
14. Both teachers work with all students.	Y	N
15. We have successfully grouped disabled students with non-disabled peers.	Y	N
16. Both teachers participate in the instruction of the students on a daily basis.	Y	N
17. We notify each other in advance in the event of an absence.	Y	N
18. Both teachers remain in the classroom the entire class period.	Y	N
19. We share parental contact responsibilities.	Y	N
20. We consistently address the class as "we" instead of "I".	Y	N

CO-TEACHING EVALUATION FORM con't

21. **Both names are listed on written correspondence. (syllabi, notes to parents, schedules, newsletters, etc.)**   Y   N

22. **Each teacher has a designated place or area in the classroom in which to keep meterials.**   Y   N

23. **Students see us as equal teaching partners.**   Y   N

24. **Administrators see us as equal teaching partners.**   Y   N

List 3 strengths of your co-teaching partnership.

1. _____

2. _____

3. _____

List 2 ideas for improvement in your co-taught class during the next grading period.

1. _____

2. _____

CO-TEACHING INTEREST INVENTORY

TO:_____

FROM:_____

RETURN TO: _____RETURN BY:_____

Please help us plan for co-taught classes by completing this information.

Grade level/subjects: _____

1. Do you currently have students with IEPs in your class?

    ☐ Yes   ☐ No

2. Would you be interested in co-teaching?

    ☐ Yes   ☐ No

3. Do you have any co-teaching experience?

    ☐ Yes   ☐ No

    If yes, please explain_____

    _____

    _____

    _____

4. Would you attend co-teaching training?

    ☐ Yes   ☐ No

Co-Teaching Lesson Plan - Daily

Date and Standard	Co-Teaching Model	Lesson	Materials	Assessment	Homework	• Modifications • Accommodations • Enrichment

IC - *Instruct, Circulate*   **IO** - *Instruct, Observe*   **R** - *Rotation*   **P** - *Parallel*   **LS** - *Large Group/Small Group*   **T** - *Team*

Co-Teaching Lesson Plan - Weekly

Subject: _____

Period/Time: _____

Co-Teachers: _____

Week of: _____

Date and Standard	Co-Teaching Model	Lesson	Materials	Assessment	Homework	• Modifications • Accommodations • Enrichment
Monday						
Tuesday						
Wednesday						
Thursday						
Friday						

IC - *Instruct, Circulate*   **IO** - *Instruct, Observe*   **R** - *Rotation*   **P** - *Parallel*   **LS** - *Large Group/Small Group*   **T** - *Team*

CO-TEACHING OBSERVATION FORM/FORMAL

Co-Teacher _____ Co-Teacher _____

Subject _____ Grade _____

Observer _____

Date and Time of Observation_____ Date and Time of Follow-up Conference_____

It is recommended that both co-teachers receive a copy of this form in a pre-observation conference. At that time, the observer should inform the teachers on how this form will be used. Note: Every element listed may not be observed during one lesson. A co-teaching relationship develops gradually and is based on mutual trust and respect. Co-teachers continually develop their skills as they work with each other.

0 - not observed   1 - somewhat evident   2 - clearly evident

I. PLANNING/PREPARATION

A. Both teachers can provide evidence of parity. (a desk or place for each teacher to keep materials, both names on materials sent home, on class rosters, syllabi, newsletters, on the door, etc.)	**0**	**1**	**2**
B. Both teachers can provide the most recent completed copy of the **Co-Teaching Evaluation Form,** page 72.	**0**	**1**	**2**
C. Both teachers can provide a copy of IEP accommodations/modifications for students in their class.	**0**	**1**	**2**
D. Both teachers were involved in the development of the lesson plan.	**0**	**1**	**2**

CO-TEACHING OBSERVATION FORM con't.

0 - not observed   1 - somewhat evident   2 - clearly evident

I. PLANNING/PREPARATION, con't

The lesson plan includes:

E. Appropriate academic standards and objectives for lessons consistent with the state's curriculum guidelines	0	1	2
F. Use of more than one way of co-teaching (refer to **Ways to Co-Teach Quick Reference**, page 79)	0	1	2
G. Planning for varied instructional strategies	0	1	2
H. Evidence that both teachers will be actively involved with instruction	0	1	2
I. Evidence of adaptations for individual student's needs (both enrichment and remediation)	0	1	2
J. Evidence of accommodations/modifications	0	1	2
K. Appropriate and clear assessments of student learning with adaptations, as needed	0	1	2

II. CLIMATE FOR LEARNING

Both teachers' performance demonstrates a shared responsibility for:

A. Classroom rules and procedures resulting in effective use of instructional time	0	1	2
B. Effective management of classroom behavior	0	1	2
C. Promoting and modeling respectful interaction among the students, between teachers and students and between the co-teachers	0	1	2
D. Communicating high expectations for all students through support and encouragement	0	1	2
E. Ensuring that all students are engaged in meaningful work throughout the class time	0	1	2
F. Both teachers work with all students; the classroom environment would make it difficult to identify students with disabilities from their non-disabled peers.	0	1	2

CO-TEACHING OBSERVATION FORM con't.

0 - not observed   1 - somewhat evident   2 - clearly evident

III. INSTRUCTIONAL PRACTICES

During instruction, both teachers:

A. Use "we" and "us" instead of "I" and "my"	**0**	**1**	**2**
B. Are actively involved in the instruction of all students with communication and instruction flowing freely between the co-teachers	**0**	**1**	**2**
C. Use a variety of instructional strategies to promote the success of all students ☐ individualized instruction ☐ grouping strategies (refer to **Ways to Co-Teach Quick Reference** listed below) ☐ manipulatives/technology ☐ projects ☐ peer teaching ☐ direct instruction ☐ other_____	**0**	**1**	**2**

WAYS TO CO-TEACH QUICK REFERENCE

One Instructs, One Circulates (I,C)
Teacher A manages the overall classroom and oversees instruction. Teacher B circulates answering questions, getting the attention of students back on lesson, helping an individual, etc.

One Instructs, One Observes (I,O)
One teacher manages the overall classroom and oversees instruction. The other teacher plays a passive role, but is observing one student, a group of students or even the whole class for a specific purpose of gaining information and for a specific amount of time. This information will be analyzed together.

Rotation (R)
Students rotate through stations. Teacher A works at one station presenting information or an activity. Teacher B works at another station presenting different information or activity. One station is for independent work.

Parallel (P)
Co-teachers are both teaching the same information, but they divide the class.

Large Group, Small Group (L,S)
The class is divided. Teacher A instructs a large group in a planned lesson and Teacher B leads a small group in another lesson or the same lesson taught at a different level or for a different purpose.

Team (T)
Both teachers are active instructors. They work together to instruct the entire class. Conversation and presentation of the lesson flow seemlessly between the teachers.

CO-TEACHING OBSERVATION FORM con't.

0 - not observed   1 - somewhat evident   2 - clearly evident

III. INSTRUCTIONAL PRACTICES

During instruction, both teachers:

D. Provide guided practice (i.e. modeling note-taking during instruction)	0	1	2
E. Move about the classroom	0	1	2
F. Assist students with and without disabilities	0	1	2
G. Adapt the instruction to a variety of learning styles (visual, auditory, kinesthetic, tactile)	0	1	2
H. Know the content of the lesson	0	1	2
I. Are comfortable with their presentation of the content	0	1	2
J. Group students with disabilities with their non-disabled peers	0	1	2
K. Re-teach students who need extra help	0	1	2
L. Provide materials that are adapted to meet individual student needs	0	1	2
M. Demonstrate appropriate pacing of instruction	0	1	2
N. Provide accommodations/modifications for students as needed	0	1	2
O. Ask a variety of questions using higher order thinking skills	0	1	2

IV. ONGOING ASSESSMENT STRATEGIES

The co-teachers use a variety of ongoing assessment strategies to fairly and accurately evaluate the real learning of the students. These may include: ☐ intervention activities to re-teach objectives ☐ group or individual questioning ☐ teacher-made and standardized quizzes/tests with appropriate adaptations and accommodations ☐ students working at the board ☐ written or oral assignments ☐ projects ☐ labs ☐ other _____	0	1	2

Follow Up Conference and Signatures

_____
Teacher's Signature and Date

_____
Teacher's Signature and Date

_____
Observer's Signature and Date

CO-TEACHING OBSERVATION FORM/INFORMAL
(SIX IN SIX MINUTES)

Observer _____ Date_____

Co-Teachers _____Co-Teachers _____

NOTES FROM OBSERVATION

0 - not observed	1 - somewhat evident	2 - clearly evident			
			0	**1**	**2**

I. Co-teachers have planned together.

                                                           0   **1**   **2**

2. Teachers use "we" and/or "us."   **0**   **1**   **2**

3. Both teachers are involved in instruction.   **0**   **1**   **2**

4. Students are engaged in learning.   **0**   **1**   **2**

5. Both teachers work with all students.

6. Ways to co-teach observed:

☐ One instructs, one circulates

☐ One instructs, one observes

☐ Rotation

☐ Parallel

☐ Small group. large grojup

☐ Teaming

Additional Notes:

CO-TEACHING PARENT LETTER

Dear Parent/Guardian,

We are excited to have your student in our co-taught Language Arts class this year. This course will be instructed by two certified, professional teachers, working together to meet the diverse needs of <u>all</u> our students. With large class sizes and diverse learning styles, two teachers in a classroom will benefit everyone! Since we are both in the classroom to serve all students, your child will have a teacher available to assist them. We will meet together to plan lessons for your child that will be educational, active, engaging and creative. We will co-plan, instruct and assess the students together. We will implement a number of teaching strategies and styles into our lessons. We invite you to observe the class at any time. Please let us know of any questions or concerns regarding your student.

Sincerely,

Mrs. Sampson   Mrs. Davidson
ssampson@email.com   jdavidson@email.com
555-5643 ext 231   555-5643 ext 243
Planning period – block 6   Planning period – block 4

CO-TEACHING WORKSHEET

It is recommended that both teachers complete this worksheet together <u>prior</u> to their co-teaching experience. Reviewing procedural matters now will help to avoid miscommunication and frustration that may arise during the school year.

1. Discuss your philosophy about teaching students with special needs in a general education classroom.

    _____

    _____

    _____

2. Explain your interest in co-teaching.

    _____

    _____

    _____

3. Share some of the co-teaching responsibilities you would like to have.

    _____

    _____

    _____

4. Discuss your biggest concern(s) about co-teaching.

    _____

    _____

    _____

5. What are your goals for this co-taught class?

    _____

    _____

    _____

6. Negotiate instructional expectations. Discuss the standards, the scope and sequence, and pacing for the course. **Note:** Each co-teacher should be provided a copy of the course standards and a teacher's edition of the textbook.

    _____

    _____

    _____

CO-TEACHING WORKSHEET con't

7. List all correspondence which will use both teachers' names. **Example:** notes to parents, newsletters, syllabi, schedules, report cards, etc.

_____

_____

_____

8. Decide on a designated place or desk for the co-teacher (coming into the classroom) to keep his/her materials.

_____

_____

_____

9. How will parents be informed that their student will be in a co-taught class? (See **Co-Teaching Parent Letter,** page 82)

_____

_____

_____

10. How will each of you be introduced to the students? What can you do to convey to the students that two professional teachers are in the classroom working together? **Example:** the use of "we" instead of "I"

_____

_____

_____

11. How will parental contacts be made? **Example:** Who will return phone calls and e-mails, attend parent/teacher conferences, and so forth?

_____

_____

_____

12. How will IEP accommodations/modifications be monitored? Where will the information about the students' accommodations/modifications be kept? **Example:** specified binder, grade book, file folder, etc.

_____

_____

_____

CO-TEACHING WORKSHEET con't

13. How and when will you plan? *This time is very important, so schedule now before your calendars are full.* (See **Finding Time to Plan,** page 30).

_____

_____

_____

14. What are your pet peeves? We all have a least one! **Example:** If you do not want students to use pens on quizzes and tests, state it; if you cannot stand students chewing gum in class, let it be known.

_____

_____

_____

15. How will you notify your co-teacher that you will be absent? What will the substitute be expected to do? **Note:** An absent co-teacher should always be provided a substitute. This substitute should not be pulled from a co-taught class to cover another class.

_____

_____

_____

16. Discuss paperwork responsibilities. These may include:

   • attendance procedures _____

   • discipline referrals _____

   • progress reports/newsletters to parents _____

   • bulletin boards _____

   • copying papers _____

   • other _____

17. Discuss the grading and recording of written assignments, quizzes and tests.

_____

_____

_____

CO-TEACHING WORKSHEET con't

18. Discuss classroom rules and how they will be enforced.

_____

_____

_____

19. Discuss daily class routines and procedures for students:

   • leaving the class for water and restroom_____

   • late to class _____

   • asking questions in class _____

   • turning in written assignments _____

   • sharpening pencils_____

   • lining up (elementary) _____

   • walking down the hall (elementary) _____

   • taking make-up quizzes and tests _____

   • getting missed assignments_____

   • turning in late assignments _____

   • transitioning within classroom (noise level) _____

20. Discuss the acquisition and utilization of supplies and equipment needed for the classroom.

_____

_____

_____

21. How will you resolve differences? Some differences of opinion are normal. **Have a plan to communicate concerns while they are still small.**

_____

_____

_____

22. Schedule a date each grading period to complete an evaluation. Discuss the results and adjust as needed. (See **Co-Teaching Evaluation,** pages 72-73)

_____

_____

_____

DAILY MONITORING REPORT

Name:_____Date: _____

Class: _____Teacher: _____

Return to: _____

Please check **Yes** or **No** for each statement and sign daily.

	MONDAY		TUESDAY		WEDNESDAY		THURSDAY		FRIDAY	
	YES	NO	YES	NO	YES	NO	YES	NO	YES	NO
BRINGS ALL MATERIALS										
HOMEWORK COMPLETED										
STAYS ON TASK										
CLASSWORK COMPLETED										
APPROPRIATE BEHAVIOR										
TEACHER'S SIGNATURE										

Comments: _____

_____

_____

_____

_____

DAILY OBSERVATIONS

Name: _____

Class: _____Period: _____Teacher: _____

Return to: _____Return by: _____

Date:_____

Date:_____

Date:_____

Date:_____

Date:_____

DOCUMENTATION OF PARENTAL CONTACT

Student: _____Phone _____

Parent's Name:_____

<table>
<tr><td align="center">DATE</td><td align="center">REASON FOR CONTACT</td></tr>
<tr><td>1. _____</td><td>1. _____
_____
_____</td></tr>
<tr><td>2. _____</td><td>2. _____
_____
_____</td></tr>
<tr><td>3. _____</td><td>3. _____
_____
_____</td></tr>
<tr><td>4. _____</td><td>4. _____
_____
_____</td></tr>
<tr><td>5. _____</td><td>5. _____
_____
_____</td></tr>
<tr><td>6. _____</td><td>6. _____
_____
_____</td></tr>
</table>

HOMEWORK ASSIGNMENTS

Student: _____ Week of: _____

DATES	(subject)	(subject)	(subject)	(subject)	(subject)	(subject)
MONDAY	☐ COMPLETED	☐ COMPLETED	☐ COMPLETED	☐ COMPLETED	☐ COMPLETED	☐ COMPLETED
TUESDAY	☐ COMPLETED	☐ COMPLETED	☐ COMPLETED	☐ COMPLETED	☐ COMPLETED	☐ COMPLETED
WEDNESDAY	☐ COMPLETED	☐ COMPLETED	☐ COMPLETED	☐ COMPLETED	☐ COMPLETED	☐ COMPLETED
THURSDAY	☐ COMPLETED	☐ COMPLETED	☐ COMPLETED	☐ COMPLETED	☐ COMPLETED	☐ COMPLETED
FRIDAY	☐ COMPLETED	☐ COMPLETED	☐ COMPLETED	☐ COMPLETED	☐ COMPLETED	☐ COMPLETED
NEXT TEST DATE						

IEP ANNUAL REVIEW PROGRESS REPORT

Student: _____

Subject/Teacher: _____

IEP Case Manager: _____

Date Sent:_____   Return by: _____

I will be holding an annual IEP review on this student. In order to review his/her progress and develop a new IEP, your input, suggestions and recommendations would be helpful.

Please complete the following information on this student's classroom performance.

COMMENTS ON ACADEMIC AND BEHAVIOR PROGRESS: _____

_____

_____

_____

_____

_____

_____

RECOMMENDATIONS: _____

_____

_____

_____

_____

_____

_____

Your assistance and cooperation are sincerely appreciated!

IEP CLASSROOM ACCOMMODATIONS/MODIFICATIONS

To the teachers of: _____

From: _____IEP Case Manager

Date:_____

RE: <u>Accommodations/Modifications in the General Education Classroom</u>

Teachers:
To comply with the IEP, certain accommodations and modifications must be followed. This student needs the accommodations and modifications listed below. I am available to answer any questions you may have. Please inform me of any problems that may arise with this student. Thank you for your assistance.

Planning Period_____Room #_____

Accommodations/Modifications as stated on the IEP:

1. _____

2. _____

3. _____

4. _____

5. _____

Accommodations/Modifications to the Discipline Policy: (Please refer to the attached Behavior Intervention Plan):

1. _____

2. _____

3. _____

INTRODUCTION TO PARENT LETTER

Dear Parents:

It is a pleasure to be _____'s IEP case manager this year at _____. I look forward to working with you and your child to ensure a successful school year.

I am enclosing a sample progress report which will be used to monitor your child's progress in all subject areas. Copies of these progress reports will be mailed to you after I review them with your child.

Please feel free to call me if you have any questions or concerns or if you feel we need to schedule a conference with your child's teacher(s). The school telephone number is _____.

It is my privilege to be working with you this year. Together we can make it a year of growth and learning.

Sincerely,

Special Education Teacher

NOTEBOOK ORGANIZATION POINT SHEET

Name _____

Date _____

Criteria: Notebook present _____
(25 points)

Criteria: Dates on work _____
(20 points)

Criteria: Pages in order _____
(20 points)

Criteria: All papers secure _____
(10 points)

Criteria: Study skills noted _____
(25 points)

Total score: _____/100 points

Comments: _____

_____

_____

Name _____

Date _____

Criteria: Notebook present _____
(25 points)

Criteria: Dates on work _____
(20 points)

Criteria: Pages in order _____
(20 points)

Criteria: All papers secure _____
(10 points)

Criteria: Study skills noted _____
(25 points)

Total score: _____/100 points

Comments: _____

_____

_____

Name _____

Date _____

Criteria: Notebook present _____
(25 points)

Criteria: Dates on work _____
(20 points)

Criteria: Pages in order _____
(20 points)

Criteria: All papers secure _____
(10 points)

Criteria: Study skills noted _____
(25 points)

Total score: _____/100 points

Comments: _____

_____

_____

Name _____

Date _____

Criteria: Notebook present _____
(25 points)

Criteria: Dates on work _____
(20 points)

Criteria: Pages in order _____
(20 points)

Criteria: All papers secure _____
(10 points)

Criteria: Study skills noted _____
(25 points)

Total score: _____/100 points

Comments: _____

_____

_____

NOTIFICATION OF PARENT MEETING

To: _____Dept.: _____

From: _____IEP Case Manager

Date: _____Return Date: _____

Name of student: _____

The parent(s) of _____ have requested a meeting to

discuss his/her educational program.

    Meeting Date: _____

    Time: _____

    Location: _____

Please return the bottom portion of this letter to my mailbox by _____

indicating if you will be in attendance.

Thank you.

Student's Name:_____

   ☐ Yes, I will attend the meeting.

   ☐ No, I will be unable to attend the meeting.

Signature:_____

PROGRESS REPORT FOR PARENTS

Student's Name: _____Date: _____

Subject: _____Teacher:_____

Return to:_____

_____'s parents have requested an update of _____'s progress in each of his/her classes.

1. At this time the level of achievement of this student seems to be:

    ☐ increasing   ☐ decreasing   ☐ remaining the same

2. List any assignments which are due or past due:

    _____

    _____

    _____

2. List any major assignments/projects the student should be working on:

    _____

    _____

    _____

4. The items checked below are suggested as needing improvement:

    ☐ Attendance

    ☐ Bringing materials to class

    ☐ Completing work on time

    ☐ Attentive and actively participating

    ☐ Working independently

    ☐ Effort (the student displays little interest in learning)

    ☐ Preparing for tests

    ☐ Negative or disruptive behavior

REQUEST FOR CONSULTATION FORM
(to be completed by general education teacher)

Name of Student: _____ Period: _____

Faculty Member Making Request: _____

Subject: _____

Date of Request: _____

REQUESTED SERVICE	DATE NEEDED

FOR CONSULTANT'S USE ONLY

Date of Consultation with Student/Teacher _____

Service Provided: _____

_____

_____

_____

_____

_____

REQUEST FOR CONSULTATION LETTER

TO:

DATE:

FROM: **LEARNING STRATEGIES DEPARTMENT**

CONSULTATION

The goal of consultation is to assist classroom teachers to provide successful learning experiences for students with special needs. We are available to assist with adjustments in pacing, method of instruction, special materials/techniques, and performance standards. We can provide assistance with IEP accommodations/modifications.

If you need assistance with any special education student in your class, please use the **Request for Consultation Form** to request our services.

STUDENT INFORMATION SHEET

Student's Name: _____

Address: _____

Home Phone _____

Birthdate: _____

Grade: _____

Parent or Guardian's Name: _____

Work/Cell Phone Number: Mother: _____

                                                     Father: _____

Place of Employment: Mother: _____

                                            Father: _____

E-Mail Address: Mother: _____

                                    Father: _____

STUDENT PROGRESS REPORT

Teacher: _____Class: _____

Student: _____Date Return:_____

IEP Case Manager: _____

1. Upcoming tests or projects:

_____

_____

_____

2. Missed assignments that can be made up:

_____

_____

_____

3. Items needing improvement:

	IMPROVEMENT NEEDED	COMMENTS
ABSENCES OR TARDIES		
BRINGING MATERIALS TO CLASS		
EFFORT		
NEGATIVE OR DISRUPTIVE BEHAVIOR		
HOMEWORK COMPLETION		
OTHER		

SUPPORT CLASS PROGRAM EVALUATION

(to be completed by students)

1. Do you feel you are getting the help you need?

   ☐ Yes   ☐ No

   Explain _____

   _____

2. What do you like about the Support Class? _____

   _____

   _____

   _____

3. Which of these units helped you?
   - ☐ Time management
   - ☐ Organization skills
   - ☐ Test taking skills
   - ☐ Parts of textbook
   - ☐ SQR3
   - ☐ Career explorations
   - ☐ Note taking skills
   - ☐ Listening skills
   - ☐ Following directions
   - ☐ Outlining skills
   - ☐ Other (Please explain) _____

   _____

2. How would you improve the class? _____

   _____

   _____

   _____

TEST PREPARATION FORM

*(to be completed by student **prior** to teacher signature)*

Name: _____

Subject: _____

Test Date: _____

Ask and Answer the following questions. Have your subject teacher sign this sheet once it has been completed.

1. What materials will be covered on the test?

   _____

   _____

2. What should you do to prepare for the test?

   Study old quizzes? _____

   Study class notes? _____

   Read material in book? _____

   Read/do chapter reviews?_____

3. Will there be a review before the test? ☐ Yes ☐ No

   If so, when will the review be? _____

4. Will you have a study guide? _____

5. What type of test will it be?
   ☐ Multiple Choice
   ☐ True/False
   ☐ Short Answer
   ☐ Fill in the Blanks
   ☐ Essay
   ☐ Other

Signature of teacher: _____

WEEKLY ASSIGNMENTS

To: _____ Subject: _____

From: _____ Return Date:_____

_____ is in my support class. In order to monitor his/her academic progress, please complete the following information. If you have suggestions or other ways in which I can help reinforce what you are doing in the classroom, please let me know.

For the week of:_____

	HOMEWORK ASSIGNMENTS	READING ASSIGNMENTS	REVIEW	TEST	PROJECT	OTHER
MONDAY						
TUESDAY						
WEDNESDAY						
THURSDAY						
FRIDAY						

Would you like a conference? ☐ Yes   ☐ No

Additional Comments: _____

_____

WEEKLY PROGRESS REPORT

Subject:_____   Week of: _____

_____   Student:_____

TEACHER'S SIGNATURE

All homework completed   ☐ Yes   ☐ No

Comments_____

_____

All classwork completed   ☐ Yes   ☐ No

Comments_____

_____

Appropriate behavior   ☐ Yes   ☐ No

Comments_____

_____

Test Grade (if applicable) _____

All homework completed   ☐ Yes   ☐ No

Comments_____

Subject:_____

_____

_____

TEACHER'S SIGNATURE

___All classwork completed   ☐ Yes   ☐ No

Comments_____

_____

Appropriate behavior   ☐ Yes   ☐ No

Comments_____

_____

Test Grade (if applicable) _____

All homework completed   ☐ Yes   ☐ No

Comments_____

Subject:_____

_____

_____

TEACHER'S SIGNATURE

___All classwork completed   ☐ Yes   ☐ No

Comments_____

_____

Appropriate behavior   ☐ Yes   ☐ No

Comments_____

_____

Test Grade (if applicable) _____

REFERENCES

Basso, D. & McCoy, N. (1996). *Study Skills: A comprehensive curriculum guide for teaching study skills to students with special needs.* Columbia, SC: Twins Publications.

Cook, L., & Friend, M. (1995). Co-Teaching: Guidelines for creating effective practices. *Focus on Exceptional Children, 28 (3), 1-16.*

DeBoer, A. & Fister,S. (1989). 24 easy techniques to guarantee the failure of educational partnerships. *Special Educator, January.*

Freytag, C. (2003). *Factors influencing secondary co-teachers' perceptions of co-teaching: A path analytic model.* Unpublished doctoral dissertation, University of Central Florida, Orlando.

Friend, M., & Cook, L. (2003) *Interactions: Collaboration skills for school professionals (4th ed).* Boston, MA: Allyn and Bacon.

Salend, S.J. (2005). *Creating inclusive classrooms: Effective and reflective practices for all students (5th ed.).* Columbus, OH: Merrill/Prentice Hall.

WEB SITES

www.twinspublications.com
(Co-teaching and study skills curriculum, co-teaching training)

www.ldonline.org
(Learning disability resource for teacher and parents)

www.powerof2.org
(Articles about collaboration in inclusive classroom)

www.4teachers.org
(Web resources for teachers)

www.circleofinclusion.org
(Early childhood information for inclusion programs.)

www.ldinfo.com
(Resource for teachers and parents including learning disabilities and emotional behaviors)

www.specialconnections.ku.edu.
(University of Kansas - collaboration articles)

Co-Teaching Training

by Dianne Basso & Natalie McCoy

Are the requirements in No Child Left Behind (NCLB) and IDEA 2004 regarding highly qualified teachers impacting your district? Are you interested in receiving more information about Co-Teaching, an effective service delivery model for increasing the achievement of students with disabilities while also meeting the needs of diverse learners in the general education classroom?

Dianne Basso and Natalie McCoy provide Co-Teaching training for teachers and administrators. They are teachers and nationally recognized consultants, presenters and authors with hands-on experience in co-teaching and inclusion. They are the authors of *The Co-Teaching Manual and Study Tools: A Comprehensive Study Skills Curriculum*. These books are designed to increase the effectiveness of inclusion programs.

During the training, Dianne and Natalie model co-teaching strategies and techniques for co-teachers and administrators. Some of the topics covered are:

- Definition of Co-Teaching
- Specific ideas for defining roles and responsibilities of co-teachers and administrators
- Benefits of a successful co-teaching program
- Creative ways to find time to plan
- A variety of ways to present curriculum in a co-taught classroom
- Scheduling options for a co-taught classroom
- Techniques for providing instruction in a co-taught classroom for teachers and administrators

In addition to initial Co-Teaching training, Dianne and Natalie offer follow-up training, classroom observations and co-teaching program support.

"The Co-Teaching Manual is a valuable resource for our teachers. Natalie and Dianne are great speakers. They shared a lot of practical information that teachers can start using tomorrow!"

—ADMINISTRATOR, PENNSYLVANIA

"This was one of the most useful in-services I have ever been to. I like the way Dianne and Natalie present using what they teach. They really "model" co-teaching.

—REGULAR EDUCATION TEACHER, NORTHWEST OHIO SCHOOLS

"This was my first exposure to the co-teaching concept. I gained relevant, useful information that I will use. I don't like to be out of my classroom for workshops, but this training proved to be worth it for my students and me. We will all benefit from this training.

—SPECIAL EDUCATION TEACHER, WEST VIRGINIA

For more information visit our website:
www.twinspublications.com or call us at (803) 782-1781

Twins Publications Order Form

P.O. Box 6364
Columbia, SC 29260-6364
(803) 782-1781 • Fax (803) 787-8508
www.twinspublications.com

TWINS
publications

Teachers Writing For Teachers

Other books by Dianne Basso & Natalie McCoy

Study Tools
(364 pages)

This comprehensive study skills curriculum offers helpful strategies for students covering topics such as organization, note taking skills, test-taking skills, time management, memory, listening, writing, and using SQ3R. The curriculum includes lesson plans, worksheets, tests, and answer keys.

3 WAYS TO ORDER:

1. Order online by credit card 24 hours a day @ www.twinspublications.com
2. Mail order form and send check to:
   Twins Publications, PO Box 6364, Columbia, SC 29260-6364
3. Send purchase order or fax to 803.787.8508

ITEM	QTY.	PRICE	AMOUNT
The Co-Teaching Manual	_____	$32.95	_____
Study Tools	_____	$89.95	_____
		SUBTOTAL	_____
	10 % SHIPPING & HANDLING (USA)		_____
	(outside of USA, please call)		
	SALES TAX (if applicable)		_____
		TOTAL	_____

BILL TO:

Name: _____

Facility: _____

Address: _____

City, State, Zip _____

Phone: (_____) _____

SHIP TO:

Name: _____

Facility: _____

Address: _____

City, State, Zip _____

Phone: (_____) _____